We Before Me

price / quote good for ten
days —
Update templates?

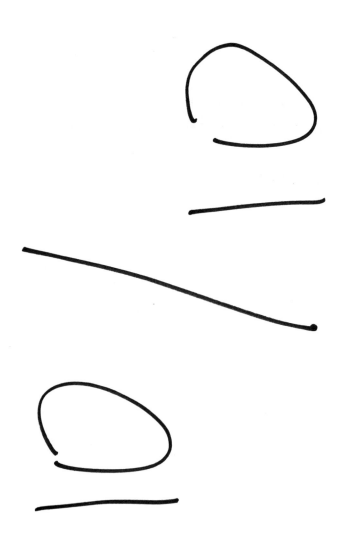

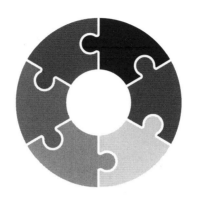

WE BEFORE ME

BUILDING A TEAM GREATER
THAN THE SUM OF ITS PARTS

———

MICHAEL GILPIN

credo
house publishers

Published in the United States of America by Credo House Publishers
a division of Credo Communications LLC, Grand Rapids, Michigan
credohousepublishers.com

ISBN: 978-1-62586-233-4

Interior design and typesetting by Believe Book Design LLC
Editing by Michael A. Vander Klipp

Printed in the United States of America

First edition

To my incredible wife, Erin.

The story we have built at FASTSIGNS would have been impossible without your consistent and unwavering support. Thank you for the encouragement to share our story.

Contents

CHAPTER 1

WE KNEW OUR "WHY?"

THE NURSERY HAD A CHAIR RAIL going all the way around the room. We had decided on a sky blue to be painted above the rail and a sage green below. We went with fairly neutral colors, as we didn't know the gender of the baby, but wanted to get the nursery prepped and ready for our first child, who was due in June of 2005. Everything was going to plan.

My job transferred us from Grand Rapids, Michigan to Allentown, Pennsylvania back in 2003. My side of the family lived in Michigan; my wife Erin has family in Ohio. With no family or friends out in eastern Pennsylvania, we entered a new adventure for both of us.

Two years post transfer, my career was moving right along as the General Manager of a foam fabrication manufacturing plant. It had gone so well, I had a promotion sitting on my desk to consider. Erin had a great career as well, working for a large, prominent insurance company. As a math and statistics major, she utilized her education quite well as a product and data analyst. So with third wedding anniversary approaching, our first child due within the next few months, both careers going well, and amazing friendships established, I would say we had hit our groove. While there was plenty of unexpected on the horizon as we were soon to be first-time parents, everything else was pretty stable.

As I dipped my roller into the blue paint to apply another coat to the top section of the wall, the phone rang. It was my dad. After a few pleasantries, he asked me a very simple question. "Do you think you're ready to start up a family business?"

In fairness, I was anticipating this question at some point in my life. My dad and I both shared the same values, loved business, and we'd had a chance to work together a little in the past so we knew a father/son business partnership was a viable option for us. But now?

I turned to Erin and repeated the question to her with my dad still on the phone. Without hesitation she started swinging her head left to right in a manner that didn't just say "no," it said, "ABSOLUTELY NOT!" I questioned my dad by asking about the timing, to which he responded with an explanation that he was "no spring chicken." I guess I had pictured being fully established for twenty years or so before starting a family business. After all, that was what my dad was doing. After an amazing career with a fortune 500 company, he managed to retire (for the first time) at the ripe old age of 47. For some reason, it never really dawned on me that when I would be 47, my dad would be 74. I could sense that he wasn't exactly wanting to wait until his 74th birthday to open a new business.

"Why?"

So, with the question on the table, my wife challenged me with three simple little letters, combined to make one powerful question: "Why?" This question was raised not in an angry or frustrated tone, but in an honest and authentic way, seeking a heartfelt answer. Why would my dad and I want to start up a family business? What could be gained by leaving a great career with a company I liked to start something from nothing? What would be worth the risk of leaving a secure job to enter the unknown, especially when our first child would be here within weeks?

While we didn't know what the family business would be at this point in the conversation, we were pretty confident it wouldn't be based in Allentown. That would mean not only entering the world of the unknown for career and financial security, but doing it at the same time as having our first child and shortly after moving 700 miles. That seemed like quite the overwhelming set of tasks to take on. Any one of these alone is enough of a life change to warrant just a little bit of stress; taken together, it's a lot to consider.

This is probably a good time to mention the fact that my amazing wife has some specific characteristics about her. She is the most loving, unselfish, encouraging and beautiful person I know. In addition, she is not a big fan of change; she struggles with the unknown, and having a sense of security is high on her list of things she desires. So, getting an answer to her simple question of "why" was critical for her to understand for a variety of reasons. The answer, "I've always wanted to start a business with my dad" was not going to be sufficient. I couldn't be more grateful for that answer not being sufficient for her, as it would have been short-sighted if it was sufficient for me. The question needed a thoughtful, authentic answer—not only for Erin, but for me as well. Why would I want to do this?

Thankfully, as we sorted out an answer to this powerful question, my dad and I were in 100 percent agreement each step of the way. While we had to put thought into our answer and formulate it into words, it was not a laborious process for us. The "why" was in our DNA. Simply stated, we wanted to build and lead a team of people that wanted to grow and give back. The goal of team growth had many facets to it: the growth of the business, the professional development of the team and its individuals, and the personal growth of each team member. The giving back had many facets to it as well: we wanted to give back to our customer base through great service and authentically caring about them as people; give back to the community we live in; and give back to each other by putting others before ourselves. So to put it in even simpler terms, we wanted to build a team, kick butt and put others first.

The first simple step was to make sure the ego was checked at the door. Both my dad and I agreed that this was not going to be about us. This was going to be about the team. From day one it was going to be "We Before Me." We wanted each of our team members to feel empowered, special, and as much of an owner of the business as we were.

Sounds simple, right? But my dad and I knew through previous interactions with many different companies that this type of company culture was not commonplace. We had a chance to build something special. By formulating an agreed-upon "why," we would be able to work through other challenges and differences that came up over the years knowing that the foundation of the business was based upon these shared values and vision.

Sharing the Why, Understanding the What

By no means was sharing the "why" one simple conversation with Erin; rather, it was a conversation that evolved into her having a good understanding of the foundation of the business we wanted to start. We had several conversations, sought advice from others, prayed and reflected, and did a great deal of due diligence. Through this fast-paced process, Erin and I came to the monumental decision that we were ready to embark on this huge life change, move back home, start a family business.

With our "why" established, we just needed to figure out one more small detail… what type of business were we going to open? While it may seem somewhat comical that we went through the process of deciding if we were going to open a business without knowing what the business would be, I cannot emphasize how critical this process of evaluation and soul-searching was. The foundation of the "why" was more important than any widget or service we could sell. We knew the type of culture we wanted to build and we knew why we wanted to build it. Now we just had to face the challenging task of figuring out what the widget or service would be.

Much like digging deep into understanding why we would want to start a family business, we had to put some parameters around the type of business we would open. While we needed to create something that would be profitable and sustainable, we also knew that we would want to work with a product or service that we could enjoy and a business that would grow. Through many conversations, we came up with the following criteria:

1. We wanted Monday through Friday operation to give team members family time on the weekends.
2. We were looking for a community-based business so we could share our products or services in the community in which we lived.
3. We wanted to manufacture a product. We both had been in the manufacturing sector and enjoyed the idea of the satisfaction people would get by seeing the product they produced with their own hands.
4. Our primary focus was to be on business-to-business relationships. This was an area of experience and enjoyment for both of us.
5. We were looking for a franchise system. We wanted to lean on the expertise of others on manufacturing a product or service and focus our efforts on building the right team to execute it well.

So after a great deal of researching, attending franchise trade shows, and speaking to several owner-operators out in the field, we made the decision and signed on the dotted line to become the 467th center in the FASTSIGNS franchise network. We were impressed with the brand, the products, the services and most importantly, the people within the FASTSIGNS network. This was the petri dish in which we were seeking to cultivate a business where "We" would come before "Me."

Plot Twist

This is where I introduce the plot twist. After we made this decision, I informed my employer that not only was I not going to take the promotion sitting on my desk for consideration, but I was turning in my resignation. Since my wife and I agreed we were going to wait to make sure we had a healthy child before packing up and moving, I was able to give my employer a couple months' notice. During that time, the president of the company approached me with a different promotion opportunity in an effort to keep me on the team. This promotion had an incredible salary increase, significant bonuses, and it would make me the president of one of the company's divisions in a very short amount of time. As a 26-year-old, I was taken aback by such an incredible offer. This promotion would literally triple the amount of money I was making at the time, and it would move us back to my hometown of Grand Rapids.

I shared all of this with my wife and her eyes widened much like mine at the significant increase in our household income. We knew that if I took this opportunity, we could live a similar lifestyle to what we were living now, but she wouldn't have to work outside of the home if she wanted to make the choice to be a stay-at-home mom.

The offer shook our world a little bit to say the least. What were we going to do?

I picked up the phone and called my dad. He answered with a simple "hello," after which I kindly informed him, "Dad, we have a problem." I explained to him the situation, and he too was very impressed with the significant new offer that was now sitting in front of me for consideration.

At this point in the FASTSIGNS process a few major milestones had already passed. The franchise deposit had been paid. The real estate was selected. The construction company was working away on the build out. And, most significantly, my dad and I had roped my mom into this crazy adventure as well. We were so far down the road, it definitely felt like there was no turning back.

After my parents had some time to discuss this new twist with each other, they gave me a call back. Their message was very simple: They decided they were not going to move forward with FASTSIGNS if I was not going to be a part of it. They also informed me that if I decided to take the new opportunity that was presented to me, there was no issue. Whether or not they could get their deposits back was insignificant to them. All they wanted was for me to have the freedom to make the best choice I could for myself and my family.

Wow! Are you kidding me? After all the time, effort and finances that went into making the decision to open a FASTSIGNS center, they were willing to stop the entire process and walk away. Talk about an incredible testimony to the "others first" mentality. The choice was mine.

Again, "Why?"

Erin and I found ourselves standing in the empty nursery that was now painted and fully furnished. I was talking through, yet again, the pros and cons of each opportunity. The decision-making process was very analytical and no stone was left unturned. Every aspect of this decision was being considered. Every potential future ramification from this decision was being envisioned.

Quite honestly, it was exhausting. At one point when I was talking myself in circles, Erin kindly interrupted to ask one magic question: "Why did you want to open a business with your mom and dad?" There she was again with those simple three letters asking that one profound question… "Why?"

Throughout all of the analysis of the options in front of me, I had been focusing mostly on the who, what, when, where and how questions. However, while I was considering my list of pros and cons and exploring the depths of the analysis from every possible angle, I was sweeping under the rug the most important question of "Why?".

With my forearm leaning on crib and looking up at the freshly painted wall, I let a deep breath out. I knew my answer in that moment. I knew my "why." We wanted to build something special that was focused on bringing a team of people around the idea of "We Before Me."

In that moment, I knew my "why" was not to triple my income. My "why" was not to gain a title of president of a division at such a young age. My "why" was not to have a paid-for company car. When I focused on the "why," what was once a monumental, exhausting decision to make suddenly became clear and simple. I remember the joy of calling my parents and letting them know, "No need to slow down, we are going to build something special together!"

So let me ask you, what do you think I would have decided if I didn't truly seek my "why" from the very beginning? We may never know, but there is a good chance I would have missed my "why." Now, let me be clear, there is no reason the principles in this book could not have been applied to the other business opportunity, but that wasn't my "why."

Whether you own your own business, are a leader within your company, or are reading this book because you aspire to be a leader within your organization, ask yourself, what is your "Why?". What impact do you want to make? Where do you want to make a difference?

You don't have to own a business to have a "why," and you don't need to leave your current job situation to go find a "why." However, there is an incredible purpose in knowing your "why" so when challenges arise and decisions are needed, you have a stake in the ground to reference that will help guide your decisions.

To this date, I still keep that offer letter in my "employee file" at the office. It is refreshing to look at it every now and then so I can remember how grateful I am that I was led to make the decision to open the 467th FASTSIGNS location.

CHAPTER 2
467

I WAS IRONING MY SHIRT and getting myself ready for the annual awards banquet at the FASTSIGNS International convention being held in Orlando, Florida. I could feel the emotion creeping in as that night was going to be a very special night. With over 700 FASTSIGNS locations worldwide, we were going to be recognized as the number 5 center in sales volume. This was the first time we had cracked the top 5, and I couldn't have been more proud of our team.

The top 5 locations received special recognition at the annual convention, which made it feel like another incredible milestone in our adventure. Two of our team members joined me for the trip down to Florida, and my parents, who had just retired from the business one year before, had made the drive over from their condo, 90 minutes west of Orlando, where they stay during the winter months.

As usual, there was great food, engaging entertainment, and many other awards being given throughout the night leading up to the presentation of the awards to the top 5. As the night progressed, I could not stop thinking about how so many people in that room did not understand why the 467th center was so different. While the top 5 award was a representation of the success we had, it paled in comparison to the true success we had realized in building a team and empowering people.

The personal and professional growth of our team members was more important than a shiny award indicating we had kicked some butt in sales. Sitting there at a convention center filled with people wanting to share best practices, I was unsure that the best of all the best practices of "developing leaders" was being shared. Was the root cause of our success known or understood by others? If not, what could I do about it?

The Team. The Team. The Team.

While the traditional practice was to have the names of the owners inscribed on the award, we had requested long before that any award we received would not have the Gilpin name engraved on the plaque. Don't get me wrong, there is nothing wrong with this. I don't look at an award with the name of the franchisee lasered into the acrylic and think, "What a jerk!" Not at all. We just knew early on that for us, the accomplishment would be grossly misrepresented if it only had the Gilpin name on it. So throughout the years we'd received awards, we kindly requested that the inscription would read "FASTSIGNS of Grand Rapids."

To some it seemed like a novelty; to others it was a little confusing; but to us, it meant a lot. Recognition and accolades needed to be reflective of what *WE* accomplished, not *ME*. But I still wasn't sure people understood. The impact that company culture can have on a team is significant, but unless they were in our space living and breathing it, could someone else really understand it? Could they grasp the concept and importance of collaboration and team building from a distance? Did it just sound like "rah-rah" team building rhetoric that didn't truly affect the success of the business?

As we were enjoying our dinner and watching as the various awards were being handed out, the time had finally come. Catherine Monson, CEO of FASTSIGNS International, began the introduction of the top 5 awards. Even while she began speaking I couldn't help but think, "People still don't get our story. They don't understand that this is not a Gilpin award, it is a team award." But as she presented, the words she spoke warmed my heart to a whole new level.

"Our 5th highest sales winner will tell you it is all about 'why' they do it. It's about their involvement in the community. It's about bringing every employee into the decision-making process. When I think about excellence, empowerment and employee involvement, this is the business that does it. And because of that, they get so much more than the sum of the individual parts. With sales of $3,333,545 from Grand Rapids, Michigan, Mike and Erin Gilpin and the FASTSIGNS of Grand Rapids team!"

She nailed it! While in this book we will unpack so much more than just what Catherine mentioned in her gracious introduction, it was clear that she "got it." She knew what made that 467th center unique. It wasn't just about being innovative, customer-oriented problem solvers with a passion and zeal to grow the business. It was more than that. Our work and our success had a purpose. It had a "why." Team members' input matters! And as a result, we are so much more successful as a team than we could ever be as individuals.

With over 700 FASTSIGNS centers in the network, there are many commonalities between franchises: We have the same marketing support; the tech department is constantly researching new equipment and materials and sharing that information to the network; and corporate business consultants are available to review financials and guide locations on decision-making processes. In addition, all branches have the same great CEO and executive team that is focused on supporting, encouraging and investing to create successful franchise locations, while at the corporate level there are some great vendor partnerships and negotiations taking place to share with the entire network.

But those are not all the commonalities. FASTSIGNS, in trying to figure out the best way to recruit new team members, partnered with a great application that streamlines the process and reaches quality candidates at a greatly reduced cost thanks to the power of the network. Finally, the company is there to help grow sales, reduce costs and help push the brand, products and services to the next level. These are not services reserved for the 467th center in Grand Rapids, Michigan. These are services available to every single center in the network.

Why 467 Stands Apart

So, if all these centers share the same great resources, why do we get so many employees from centers all over the country making the trip to Grand Rapids to spend time with our team?

Sure, there may be a few that just want to see how we produce the volume we produce, but many want to come visit to experience the team effort, collaboration and communication that is taking place on a daily basis in our location.

At our FASTSIGNS center, we recently had a visit from 5 centers from all across the country. One of the team members in particular was really interested in seeing our layout and how we manage to produce the sales volume we do in an efficient manner. That was his top priority and objective in making the trip to our center. I have stayed in contact with that individual ever since that visit, answering any questions he might have. The best part of this is that all of his questions are focused on team building, team empowerment and how to implement a better culture inside his center!

This individual and his brother are extremely knowledgeable, talented, and have run a successful center for years and years. They successfully took over the business their father started and have continued the success. The projects they do are simply amazing. Their creativity, quality and ability to deliver to their client needs represent some of the best practices and results in the network.

However, whether it is the young kids that are now part of their growing families, the constant 60- to 80-hour work weeks, or simply the duration in which they have been running at this pace, they are tired. It isn't that they don't have talented team members, but there are some things inhibiting them from transferring over some empowerment to team members. Catherine's quote, "They get so much more than the sum of the individual parts," has not applied to this center.

467 represents teamwork. It represents leadership development. It focuses on the individual and professional growth of team members more than the growth of sales or profits. It fosters an environment where not only is feedback given, but it is also pursued. 467 is experiencing the success that happens when a team of people are moving in the same direction; supporting, encouraging, holding each other accountable; putting others before themselves; and pursuing excellent service for both internal and external clients. With motivated, empowered people on the team, we can all proactively push forward with enthusiasm while we open ourselves to humbly and constantly learn new things.

Harry Truman once said, "It's amazing how much you can accomplish when it doesn't matter who gets the credit." That's the essence of 467. Seeing other centers implement some of the "467 way" into their businesses has become a great encouragement to us. We truly feel that we are making a difference.

That great feeling is one of the foundational reasons why we wanted this book to be written. Our team wanted to share our core beliefs, message, and ideas with others, and I just happened to be in the seat of the storyteller.

I don't want to make it sound like there aren't stressors, challenges, frustrations, and anxiety in operating a small business. All of those are realities that we deal with on a regular basis. The strength of the team makes it much easier to navigate those challenges and feelings, and we continue to get stronger with every trial that comes our way. So while there are many feelings I have as a small business owner, being tired is not one of them.

I can't say this was always the case. There were many times when "tired" might actually have been the best word to describe me. Sometimes the stress and long hours are a necessary evil of starting a small business and building a team, but living in this kind of a situation for too long is not sustainable. If you are trying to sustain your business by doing it all yourself, or even if you're going crazy because you feel compelled to make sure you have a hand in everything going on in your business, church, nonprofit, or organization, understand that there is a better way. There's a way to build margin in your life, a way to give you the best chance of being the best version of yourself inside and outside of the business.

A Note to the Reader

Before we continue, I want to make a few things crystal clear. There are plenty of FASTSIGNS centers throughout the world with great cultures. We aren't the only ones that understand, implement, and live the "We Before Me" concept. However, over the years there has been an overwhelming consensus among our team members that what we have is different, unique and takes team culture to a whole new level.

I also want to clarify the target audience for this book. This book is intended for anyone who is part of a team or is leading a team that wants to see individual and team growth.

Also, this book is specifically written for …. ME! You may be thinking ….wait, I thought this book was all about "We," not "Me." But yes, this book is also written for myself and our team.

Team culture is not something you "finish." Team culture is not something that you figure out and then move on to the next project. Even when you and your team are "all in" and believe in the concepts, you'll still stumble from time to time and will need to get yourself back on track. So yes, this book is also written to myself and our team as we continue to make tomorrow better than today.

Regardless of where you are on your journey, and regardless of the role you play on your existing team, my hope is this book will initiate a journey for you or perhaps come alongside you in the journey you are already on.

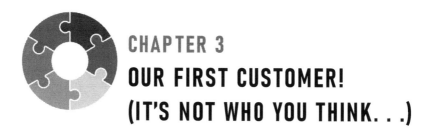

CHAPTER 3

OUR FIRST CUSTOMER!
(IT'S NOT WHO YOU THINK. . .)

OUR LITTLE FAMILY OF THREE had moved into our new home in the Grand Rapids area. The time had come to make the trip to see our FASTSIGNS location for the first time in person. My mom and dad had been moving things along in the process while Erin and I were still in Pennsylvania. They'd been keeping us updated each step of the way, but we had yet to set foot in the building.

Our physical space was still under construction, and we had seen pictures of the progress, but this would be our first time to be able to really get a good feel for where this dream of creating a business was going to take place. Needless to say, our car was filled with an incredible blend of nervousness and excitement that day.

While our branch's physical space and layout were going to be an important part of our discussion, something even more important was going to take place that day: I was going to meet our first customer face to face. I'd had the opportunity to interview Nicole over the phone, but had not had the chance to meet her face to face since she had accepted the position on our team as our first graphic designer.

You may be thinking that you just spotted a typo in the book. It says that I was able to meet our first "customer" face to face, not our "first hire" to our team. Yes, Nicole was our first team member, which also made her our first internal customer.

In traditional business practice, an interaction with a customer is focused on what you can do for them: What do they need? How can you best serve them? How can you go above and beyond to make their experience better? On the flipside, traditional practice leads to interactions with employees that focus on what they can do for you, the manager/owner.

It is very understandable why traditional thinking exists. Of course we want to go above and beyond to satisfy a customer. That's how businesses create loyal customers! Who doesn't want customers that want to send more business your way; customers that keep coming back and, when given the opportunity to talk to others, gush about the great experience they had working with you? Not only will the business grow with this kind of customer, but it will also definitely help find additional customers that may be interested in the products and services you offer.

When a business team develops an authentic relationship with the customer, they will understand that you care about them, not just their business, giving them even more reason to keep coming back to you time and time again. Of course, establishing and maintaining such great customer service means stopping what you're doing and giving them your undivided attention when they have something they want to share with you. They want to feel heard, which makes them feel important.

Sure, all this makes sense for a customer, but does it make sense for an employee? Nicole should just be happy we gave her a job, right? I mean, we're the people who are paying her; she should do what we ask and be grateful that we're giving her a paycheck. And what's with all of the questions she's asking? Here we are trying to run a business and all she gives us is nothing but interruptions and questions. If she would just do her job, then we could do ours!

Employees as Internal Customers

While many business owners might not admit it, this is the relationship they have with their employees. One minute they're bending over backward to find a way to satisfy a customer's needs, and the next they're questioning why an employee needed to leave work fifteen minutes early to pick up her sick daughter from daycare. If that customer had a sick daughter and couldn't make it to the store to pick up the product they needed for the next morning, the same owner/manager may offer to deliver the product at no additional cost and even add a little handwritten note to let them know they hope their daughter feels better soon.

Can you see the flaw in this traditional thinking? If an employee is treated like a customer, perhaps she will be the one that is excited to come in to work with you each day, be the one to tell others about her great experience, and understand that you are there to listen to her ideas, concerns and questions. I am convinced that pulling into the parking lot of your place of employment feels a lot different if you truly feel motivated, heard and important than if you are just showing up to do a job.

So let's take this even further. Let's say you have four employees on your staff. (Let me stop here a second for a quick pause to let you know that two words I cannot stand are "employee" and "staff." Just wanting to give you a hint as you continue to read that I might have a little bit of snarkiness in store when those words pop up.) For the sake of this analogy let's assume that your four employees and you serve 200 customers on a regular basis.

Now let's just say one day you had a really off day and didn't treat the customer well. You didn't deliver on a promise you made and on top of that, you didn't react well when questioned about it. Let's say you even had a little stubbornness kick in and focused on where the customer fell short in transaction. Maybe they left out a key piece of information that caused the issue. Or perhaps you made an assumption that made good common sense to you, but apparently the customer didn't agree. Whatever the situation, you aren't really feeling up to looking in the mirror and seeing where you need to take responsibility in this unfortunate situation. Regardless, it doesn't go well and you lose the customer. Now you are down to 199 customers that you serve, and you'll need to go win another one to make up for the 0.5 percent of customers you just lost.

Now transfer this concept to the way an employee is treated. After some misunderstanding between the two of you, she receives the same stubbornness and poor treatment and, much like your paying customer, she decides she doesn't want to do business with you anymore. While it is really unfortunate to lose one of your 200 customers, it is much more significant to lose 25 percent of your staff. In addition, regardless of your industry, my guess is that it is much easier and less costly to get one more customer to replace the one that you lost than it is to find a new employee. And when you find that new customer to replace one of the 200, how much training are they going to require before they can place an order with you? Likely, zero. On the flipside, once you find that employee to replace the employee that you lost, let the training begin (the assumption here is that training actually takes place!).

While it almost seems like blasphemy to claim that someone working in your business is more important than a paying customer, that's what I firmly believe is true. Don't get me wrong; we have some absolutely amazing customers, and I am extremely fortunate to have built great relationships with many of them. Many of them I don't see as "customers"; "partners" or "friends" are better terms to describe our relationship. Many of them are so supportive and encouraging they may be reading this book, so let me awkwardly reiterate in this moment that no, you are not more important than our team members. (Something tells me I might get a few text messages giving me a hard time for that statement, but I'm also confident my customers know me well enough to understand our culture and would agree that this is the way it should be.)

To be clear, just because our team members are more important, that does not diminish the fact that our customers are extremely important to us. But this is how the magic of all this happens: when the team feels important and valued and shares common vision and goals, our customers end up with better service and feel like they are our only client! So as backward as it sounds, putting team members first ends up being in the best interest of your customer.

I have heard of many situations where small business owners mention how they treat their employees really well inside their organization. They pay good wages, offer health benefits, bring in pizza on team members' birthdays and create a nice environment to work in. Setting up a motivating work environment is great, and really forms the foundation for creating a "467" culture inside an organization. Team members have a nice clean work area, the technology they are using is up to date, and the summer picnic and Christmas parties are all really nice and allow team members to have a great time.

Our First Internal Customer

Let's continue the story with our first internal customer, Nicole. Right from the start we wanted to create this type of environment for her. We had zero sales to start the business, but we wanted to make sure we offered health insurance, had a bonus program in place so we could share the team's success with her, provided holiday pay, and made sure she had updated technology and training available for her to perform her job well. While this is all great, and may be lacking in many small businesses, these are mostly environmental factors. We created a great environment for Nicole to work in.

Many people confuse "company culture" with the surroundings or environment of the workplace. A good compensation package and a clean office is a great start, but it falls short of the true potential for motivating the team and making them excited to come into work every day. In our "467" culture we wanted to see team culture rise to an entirely different level, and we decided to make this happen before we even opened our doors for the first day.

Nicole had a graphics design background and had not been out of college for too long. She had some experience working at a small print shop, so she had some familiarity with some of the things we would be doing, but really did not have experience working in the sign industry. Also, being early in her graphic design career, she definitely lacked business experience. Although lacking business experience was not a concern for us, it wasn't necessarily something that Nicole was thinking about either. She was a creative person; a graphic designer who was incredibly talented at her workstation and knew all about producing quality work. Her passion was design, not business.

On the other hand, my dad and I had a lot of business experience. Sales, marketing and operations were not only areas in which we had a lot of experience, but they were also areas of passion for us. We loved this stuff! We were all about creating opportunities, servicing customers, exceeding expectations and building a developing team to execute the plan. Operating a business was a passion of ours for so many reasons.

Want to guess what wasn't a passion of ours? Graphic design. Don't get me wrong, I thought graphic design and creativity were interesting. But to call it a passion for us as business owners was far from the truth. One of the main reasons it wasn't a passion for us was our complete lack of knowledge and understanding.

On that day when we all met for the first time together, my dad looked at Nicole and said, "If you teach us design, we will teach you the business." Seventeen years later she still remembers this statement, and seventeen years later it still means the world to her.

This one simple statement set the tone and established a couple of the core pillars in our business. First, we are in this together. We are going to learn together, and we will teach and trust each other. This was not an us (ownership) versus them (employees) environment that we were going to create. We were all in the same boat and we were going to steer it in a direction and paddle together.

The statement "If you teach us design, we will teach you the business" also carried another important pillar we established in the business: humility. We owned the business; shouldn't we be the teachers? Shouldn't we be the ones to say exactly what Nicole should do and how she should do it? No way. From day one we wanted her to know that we were excited to watch her thrive and spread her wings. We needed her to help us. And while yes, she may have felt some pressure in filling this important role, she also felt empowered to do it her way. She understood from the beginning that she was going to get the opportunity to build a business together with the owners from day one, and she knew without a shadow of a doubt that she was important. She mattered. Her thoughts, opinions, suggestions all mattered. They were heard, and they were acted upon.

Now do me a favor and just pause for a moment and think about the following. Imagine you were Nicole. Walk in her shoes. How do you feel about the "job" you are about to start? The word "job" is in quotations, because for her, it no longer was going to be a "job." It wasn't about sitting at a computer and designing nice-looking signs. Her task was bigger than that, and she was going to be an important part of growing this business. When this happens, there is a different level of excitement, a different vibe when you're pulling into the parking lot to go to work. Having a sense of ownership in the success of the business changes the team member's perspective.

The reason we welcomed Nicole in this way was very simple for us: we think it is the right way to treat people and team members. There is no alternative agenda. Ours is not a self-serving mission. The result, however, was that we welcomed a loyal person that was going to go above and beyond to help us build the business into something special. Too often organizations focus on wanting this result out of their team members, but do not establish a path for them to feel like they have a voice in the success of the organization.

What About Your Team?

Do your team members know how they impact the organization with their contributions? Do they understand why they are important to the success of the business? Do they understand how they impact profitability, customer retention, hiring and recruiting, other team members' professional development, or the overall success of the business? Reread the first question in this paragraph. Did you notice there were not any words like "key," "lead," "important," or "critical" in front of the words "team members"? All team members are important.

You might be thinking, "Well Mike, that is neat and all, but that doesn't exactly apply to all team members in my business. We have a guy who just does deliveries. And we have someone else who just receives packages. I mean, anyone can do that, so it isn't that important."

Wrong! That delivery driver is representing your organization in the final step of the sales process. Showing up on time, presenting a good image, being polite and courteous, developing a relationship with the person receiving the item being delivered—all of that makes a difference. If the driver performs his or her responsibility accurately, it impacts profitability. Being the last touch of the order with the customer gives the delivery person an opportunity to create a nice experience for the person receiving it, which creates a rapport with that individual, which reflects well upon the company. The customer can see the bright, positive attitude and recognize that this team member is different from the "average" delivery driver they see throughout the week for other products they receive. Maybe this customer starts to think of your business as a great place to work. Maybe they have a friend or family member who knows someone looking for a job, and they encourage them to check out your organization.

What's more, the delivery driver has an opportunity to provide feedback. When the delivery driver is taking the product to the customer, he can tell when something is packaged well and when it isn't. He can provide feedback to the packaging department in a constructive way to communicate how the customer perceives the presentation when it is packaged well and when it is not. The packaging department can get a better understanding of the importance of that final presentation to the customer and improve their professional development.

Does that sound like "just a driver" to you? "Just a driver" takes packages and drops them off. The end. But not everyone sees the big picture naturally. Not everyone sees how important each team member is to the entire process. And if they do not, this is an opportunity for you to coach every team member on how important they are to the process.

If they do understand their impact and are doing a great job, this is your chance to thank them and make sure they know how much of a difference they're making! If they're falling short after having the vision explained to them, it is a great opportunity to provide feedback to them. We will cover feedback in a future chapter, but before feedback can be given it is critical each team member knows how important they are to the process.

If you're not sure if they know… go ask them! Ask them how they impact the organization with the job they perform. You might get some interesting responses that will inform your team's experience in working with your organization. Remember that humility allows a business and its team members to keep learning, changing and improving.

CHAPTER 4
EXCEED, DON'T MEET

I RECEIVED THE FINISHED PHOTOS from our installers, and I couldn't have been happier.

Our local convention and visitor's bureau had placed their largest order with us that month. We had just celebrated our third year in business, and developing this relationship was very important to us. We had produced graphics for them in the past for some of their clients, but this was the first big project we did specifically for their brand. Being associated with this organization was important to us due to our mission of being involved in our community with our products and services. It was also important because this organization was well connected with many businesses, both big and small, in our community. It was a good feeling to look at the finished photos and know that we had executed the project well, and the pole banners hanging along the streets looked great.

This was a great moment of satisfaction for our team. It felt good. No, actually, it felt great.

"Mike, Mary is on the phone for you."

Ah yes, my contact at the convention and visitor's bureau must be feeling the same thing I am! I was eager to pick up the phone to share the excitement as we proudly displayed their new brand through the streets of Grand Rapids.

"Hey Mary! How are you?" I asked with enthusiasm still beaming from a job well done.

"Umm… we don't like the blue," she replied with a lot less enthusiasm. "Do you know why the blue shifted in color?"

Every once in a while there are times in business where you get the wind knocked out of your sails. I remember that moment specifically because when I answered the phone I was standing at my desk. As I heard her first statement, I slowly sat down, set my elbow on my desk and placed my palm on my forehead as I struggled to stay calm on the phone. It took everything I had to focus on the conversation as my mind was racing, wondering what had just happened. We had installed nearly $5,000 in banners and the client was not happy with the blue color that made up the entire background color on the banner! What in the world could have gone wrong?

This was not a quick fix; this was not a cheap fix. The only way to make the correction was to start over.

I continued my conversation with Mary on the phone and gathered as much information as I could. I clarified her organization's expectations of the blue color and then let her know I needed to formulate a plan to rectify the situation and I would get back to her. As I hung up the phone I felt utterly defeated. Point blank, it sucked. I had on my hands a dissatisfied customer with a financial impact that was far from favorable.

We ran a few samples of the color and compared it to the brand standards. While the blue we originally printed was close to the brand standard that was set, we were able to print some samples that matched the standard spot on. My dad and I brought over some samples and reviewed them with Mary and her team. We walked them through the process and while the blue color was very close, we admitted that we could have taken one extra step in our process to make sure it matched even closer, and we hadn't done that. We had failed.

Now, to the untrained eye, the blue color was probably close enough. Some people might say that the blues look almost the same, so what's the big deal? The big deal was that this was their new brand that they were really excited about; their organization had worked really hard to get the logo and colors just the way they wanted them, and they trusted us to execute those exact branded colors on their banners. And while anyone walking down the street noticing the new banners would probably think the blue looked really bright and good, that didn't matter. What mattered was that our client had poured months and months into their brand and was excited to see it shining bright downtown. What mattered was that we hadn't delivered to their satisfaction.

I asked Mary if we could come in and meet with her to review the next steps, and she kindly accepted my request. My dad and I made our way downtown to their office with a plan in mind. We knew we had missed the mark, but we were determined to make sure Mary and her team knew how much we valued them as a customer. We came prepared for a few different scenarios.

As we sat down with Mary, she informed us that they agreed the blue color was close, but not what they had hoped for. She also went on to say that she thought it would be a waste to reprint all of the banners. She acknowledged that most people would not know the difference, but her team was disappointed, as they had worked so hard on making color selections. We quickly informed her that we would be happy to reprint the banners with the approved sample color, but she kindly declined, again referencing that it would be a waste of material.

At that point in the conversation we let her know that we were very sorry that we had let her and her team down. We had dropped the ball on taking one extra step to verify the blue color, and we could have made a correction before all the banners were printed. After I finished acknowledging our mistake and reiterating that we knew how important it was to them to hit that color, I reached into my padfolio, pulled out a check, and handed her a full refund for the project.

She sat there in shock. She said the thought of a full refund made her uncomfortable because the banners were hanging up. They had received a good product and service; it just wasn't what they expected. I was able to explain that we were not in this relationship for an order, we were in this relationship for the long haul. We wanted to be partners for years and years to come, and it was extremely important to us to issue a refund due to the lack of satisfaction and disappointment we caused her group. It took some convincing, but she ended up accepting our refund check.

It is an honor to sit here fourteen years after that meeting and let you know we have been partners with that organization ever since. They are an incredible partner of ours, and they've been an outspoken advocate of our business and the service we provide throughout the community.

Would we still have them as a client if we hadn't issued a refund check? I don't know; maybe, maybe not. What I do know is that we decided not to take the route of meeting our client's expectations; rather, we took the route of exceeding our client's expectations. We could have easily argued that the blue color was close enough, or made the situation contentious, but we didn't. We also kept our team in the loop so they knew what type of financial decision we were going to be making and how that might impact the business.

Exceeding Expectations the 467 Way

So, yes, I will admit that this is an extreme case of exceeding the expectations of the client. However, consistently trying to exceed the expectations of our clients is one of our core values. In a competitive business environment, meeting a client's expectations are table stakes. Differentiating yourself from the competition, regardless of your industry, is rarely accomplished by simply meeting expectations. The key for us was to make sure this value was ingrained in our culture. In order to effectively exceed the expectations of the client, it needed to be a full team effort, in both the big and the little things. At 467, we needed to create an environment where exceeding expectations was the norm, not the exception.

Easy to say, but how do you do it? Maybe you have a team of people who are happy with simply meeting expectations. How do you take this to the next level? After all, if you have a team of people meeting expectations on a regular basis, it's difficult to make the case that that simply isn't enough. Standing up on a soap box explaining that their good efforts are no longer good enough is probably not the best move. Highlighting how other companies go above and beyond, and if your organization doesn't change they are going to be left in the dust… also not the best idea. Pointing out how you personally went above and beyond on a project, and demanding that others fall in line and do the same…. Yeah, that one also fits in the bad idea category. Having a meeting and listing off all the opportunities where a team member could have gone above and beyond, but didn't… you guessed it, another bad idea.

Just within the last few years, I have conducted over one hundred interviews for various positions covering every facet of our company: graphic design, sales, production and installation. Throughout the interview process, I always like to ask the question, "What motivates you?" I wish I had started keeping statistics on the answer to this question years ago, because there is one answer that stands out as the most frequent answer time and time again: "Knowing the customer was impressed with the work I did for them." While not every applicant uses these same exact words, the overall sentiment I hear over and over is that people want their customers to be really, really happy with the work they're doing.

Here's a little secret: People naturally want to exceed their client's expectations! It motivates them! It brings them joy!

So, hold on… if people want to do this, and they get joy out of making customers extremely happy, why are there so many disconnects? Why don't these desires end up with good work being done to exceed client's expectations? The answer to this question is pretty simple: Going above and beyond for the customer doesn't get noticed or celebrated internally.

Many team members feel like they're in a role where they come in on a Monday morning with a to do list longer than the time they have available to complete it, blink twice, and go home on Friday. They feel they're feverishly working away just to "keep up" with what they have in front of them.

In addition, in many business models, there are plenty of people in the process who are working together, but only a few get to experience the customer's reaction. In our business, the graphic designer and print and finishing operators are not face to face with the customer during the time of installation, pick up or delivery. So they never get answers to their questions: "Was the extra effort worth it? Did the customer react well to it?" If the answers those individuals are looking for aren't heard, there is the potential for their efforts to erode over time.

Making it Happen

So, perhaps you're the owner of a small business, or a manager of a department, and you're not seeing your team's action to exceed customer expectations taking place. You recognize that this kind of an attitude is needed to help your organization thrive, but you're not seeing that your team is motivated to change. What do you do?

This is not the time to set up a company meeting where you declare, "Starting today we are going to exceed our customers' expectations." While this desire needs to be intentional and communicated, making a blanket statement is not going to generate behavior changes. Expressing this company value needs to be organic; it needs to be lived through actions more than words. And while all of that sounds nice, you may be thinking, "How do I really make this happen?"

While there are many ways to make this happen, here are a few of our suggestions.

Check the Mirror

The first and most important step is for you to look in the mirror. What are you doing personally to exceed your customers' expectations? As a leader in your organization, pause and consider not only how you're exceeding your external customers' expectations, but also take inventory on how you have or have not been exceeding your internal customers' expectations.

Have you been so busy that you're just trying to keep up with the never-ending to-do list? Have you called a new customer to thank them for giving your company the chance to work with them, even though you may not have been personally involved in the project or transaction? What about a handwritten note of appreciation to a loyal customer? Just think, who actually receives good things in the mail these days? What a great way to make sure they know you care and appreciate them! Or have you taken the time to write a handwritten note to a team member recognizing their efforts? In most cases, those receiving the phone call or handwritten note will not be expecting it, and will be pleasantly surprised. In other words, in taking the time to thank or recognize them, you exceeded their expectations. Or maybe you're in the middle of a project, and know that if you took a few extra steps you could make the project even better for your client.

If you're already going above and beyond, great. If not, start small, start simple, but *start*. I intentionally just listed a few things that take minutes, not hours, to achieve. Even if you pick just one action and do it once a day, that activity will gain momentum and turn into a habit.

Celebrate Success

Ok, let's say you are already on board, but your team is not. Again, this is not the time for having a big company meeting in which you highlight all the ways you are exceeding customer expectations and ask why no one else is doing the same thing. My guess is that regardless of your industry, someone inside your organization is doing something to exceed an internal or external customer's expectations on a regular basis. Your mission is to find it and celebrate it!

Keep your eyes open. Keep your ears open. Look for an effort that someone is making to exceed expectations and grab ahold of it. Once you have found it, it is pretty simple. Go to the person who took the action and thank them for their extra efforts. Let them know their extra effort was appreciated and noticed. After all, this is what is going to set your organization apart—going above and beyond! Don't let a good deed go unnoticed; reinforcing this kind of behavior is critical. People like to know that their daily efforts are noticed, but people really, really like to know their exceptional, above-and-beyond efforts are noticed.

Share the Story

The next step is taking the time to share the story! When these efforts and actions take place, share them with the team.

A few things happen when the story is shared with the team. First, it reinforces the extra efforts of the individual and lets them know that their work was appreciated and noticed. Second, there are many others on the team who are trying to just make it through the day. Their to-do list is long when they show up in the morning, and somehow it is just a little bit longer when they leave at the end of the day. Hearing and seeing these stories of team members being recognized for exceeding expectations and the impact it has on the customer can help trigger a mental shift. As the sharing continues time after time, it becomes more top of mind, and those with long to-do lists have a better chance of incorporating the "extra" effort into their day.

Next, any time you receive feedback directly from the customer that highlights their expectations being exceeded, share it! And don't share it just with the person responsible for the extra effort; tell the entire team. If you are not currently getting such feedback from customers, start seeking it out through one of the many automated survey options out there. It's so easy, there truly is no reason not to gather this kind of feedback from your clients. I learn so much about our customer and our team through these survey tools. There are many times when our team members are going above and beyond I don't know about it until the customer tells me. Thanks to the customer, I find out about it and then get to celebrate it!

Once you generate a little bit of momentum, the tone of the conversation you have with your team members can change. You can highlight some examples and then really focus on why these are significant. Yes, a team member saved the day and delivered the product to the customer's hotel so they would have that rush order they needed for the trade show later that day. That's great. That's service. But paint the picture of the person who received the graphics. The one item your team member delivered is one of the many, many things they had to worry about that day. They also had a to-do list that was longer than the day would allow, and your team was able to give them peace of mind in that one area so they could complete the other items on their long list. Perhaps your team was even able to relieve some anxiety as the customer was worried about having that product or service completed in time.

When team members exceed customer expectations, the impact individuals can make on customer efforts is usually greater than they realize.

What's Next? Shut Up!

So, now that you're painting the picture and people are seeing the impact of their efforts and understanding why they are significant, you have set the stage to ask a wonderful open-ended question. "What else can we do to create a better customer experience?"

Here's the first and most important task to master once you ask the question: Shut up! Let your team members answer this question for you, rather than you supplying those answers.

You may have hundreds of ideas racing through your head of how you can exceed customer expectations and improve the customer experience. Write them down. Stick them in a folder. But most importantly, just shut up and be ready to listen!

Also realize that when you ask the question, you can't necessarily expect answers on the spot. You may have been thinking about this for a long time before posing the question, but some of the team members are getting this question sprung on them. Give them a chance to digest the question and to put some thought into answering it. By putting the question out there, you are also generating a chance for departments to have conversations about it. It also gives you a chance to have one-on-one conversations with team members to ask if they have put some thought into the question. Let them know that you are really interested in any ideas they may have. As ideas start to filter in, share those ideas with the entire team! This is where the momentum can pick up and generate more ideas.

When your team really takes this on, you get the great experience I was able to have. Our team continued to generate ideas and take on actions to give the customer a better experience. When I was able to compare their ideas to the list that I had tucked away when I decided to shut up and listen to the team, I quickly found out that their ideas were better than mine! If I would have opened my big mouth, I would have been giving out "tasks" to accomplish to go above and beyond. It would have been like I was adding to their already overwhelming to do lists.

Exceeding expectations and going above and beyond should not be a "task-related" mentality. There is a unique spirit of camaraderie that goes along with creating a better experience for another person. That spirit far exceeds a task to be crossed off a list. As I encouraged the teams to generate their own ideas, they owned and enacted those ideas, and the impact was much greater. Now, that isn't to say I didn't throw in an idea or two, but by holding back my list of actions I thought we should take on, our team and our business ended up being better and more effective in the long run.

Fast forward to seeing the benefits of fostering this kind of environment. While there are still times where we may ask the question, "How can we exceed the customer's expectations?," we do so very rarely. Very rarely. You may be wondering, "If you see it as so important, why do you so rarely ask the question? Is it because you have it all figured out and are always exceeding customer expectations?" Ha! No way! While we do well in this area, we have so much room to grow and always will. But we don't need to specifically ask the question because it is engrained into our culture.

When a new process is being implemented, team members are quick to jump in and make sure they understand the impact of this new process on the end customer. When a designer and a salesperson work on a project together, the designer will throw out questions to understand the client's expectation, but then ask questions to the salesperson trying to gauge how we can "wow" the customer with a solution. We have team members that also think this way in regard to our internal customers: Is there something they can do to make it easier for the next person in line in the process?

Excellence in this area is something we are always striving for, but it is not a separate subject anymore. It is integrated into the processes we implement internally, the products and services we offer, and in the framework of the decisions being made to help us grow.

Better Ideas, Better Team

Having a group of people striving for excellence and making efforts to exceed expectations is not what we do, it is who we are. Are we perfect? Not even close. Have we disappointed customers? Absolutely. Will we fail in the future? Guaranteed. But the culture we have will help us get through the ugly times better, we will learn along the way, and we will continue to search for and find the better, smarter, and more impactful way to serve each other and our customers.

What I have discovered is that this culture of wanting to exceed expectations internally and externally is not that common. While this helps us at 467 to stand out against the competition, it also creates a unique situation that most people do not anticipate. And if most people are not a part of a culture like this, what are the chances the new hires you bring in as the business grows have been a part of a culture like this? So far in our experience, the chances are not very good. Not at all. But getting new team members to become a part of this culture is absolutely critical.

So, how do you find the kind of people who will not only grasp the understanding of the culture, but add to it when it is not an environment they are used to? In the next chapter, I will make an effort to not only lay out some best practices we have implemented, but also help reinforce how critical it is to get it right when bringing on new team members.

Each hire is a chance to get better, not just "fill an open position."

CHAPTER 5
MORE THAN A RESUME

WE WERE GROWING AGAIN, which was
a wonderful feeling, but we needed to make our
next hire, and as always, we had to find the right
person. The area where we needed the most help
was on our production team; more specifically our
routing equipment. At the time our current operator was needed more and more in our design
department, so we needed to find more capacity
on our production team to allow this to happen.

Case Study: Tom

Enter Tom. Tom had a healthy resume.
He had been in the industry for many years; he
had spent time at several sign companies, and he
checked a lot of our hiring boxes. He was familiar
with the types of products we made, and he was
familiar with the production process. On paper
there was plenty of information to say this guy
could make a good fit for our team, but I was a
little curious as to why he had been at the number

of places he had been. His resume showed that at places he'd hung his hat at for a fairly long time, but other places not as much. He'd also gone back to a former employer at one point during his career.

So, what did I know from these pieces of information? The short answer: Nothing. I could make assumptions that Tom struggled with loyalty and bounced around. I could make assumptions that he may have had a questionable work ethic and his bouncing around wasn't voluntary on his part. I could make the assumption that he didn't get along with others and jumped ship when he wasn't happy.

There are plenty of experts out there who will teach you how to interpret a resume and what to watch out for when seeking potential employees. I tend to subscribe to the theory that assumptions like that are not worth making. Are there times when your assumptions are accurate? You bet. But choosing to follow your assumptions can create a mindset that puts a barrier between you and a potential team member if you choose not to look more deeply into the individual involved.

We had enough interest in Tom to bring him in for an interview. And, just as important, Tom had enough interest in us to want to spend some time with us to learn more about us.

Interviews are always a chance for us to share who we are to give the potential candidate a little bit of a picture of what life with us would look like. I see interviews as being like a first date: it's a chance to get to know each other and see if the relationship should continue. And much like dating, future dates only work out if both parties are interested. My hope is that this time is always well spent for both parties, and in the case of Tom it could not have been time better spent.

Tom was blown away by the cleanliness of the facility. He couldn't believe how all of the equipment was just a few years old. He couldn't believe that if something broke, our philosophy was to order whatever parts were needed to get the equipment back to working the way it should as if it were new. He couldn't believe we communicated the plan for each day to everyone. He was baffled by the thought that all departments would jump in and help if there was a big project that needed to be finished. He also was impressed with the level of trust between ownership and employees in communicating, as well as what kind of information was shared.

Quite frankly, I was blown away that Tom was blown away! Are you kidding me? Everything that he was impressed with seemed like table stakes for operating a business. As I spoke with Tom, I pried a little bit to help me understand how his experiences had been different from what he saw at 467. For the sake of being respectful to our competitors, I won't reshare the stories I heard that day. Keep in mind, Tom was being very respectful of his current and previous employers in the conversation, but he simply stated the facts of some of the hurdles that he'd typically have to overcome to complete his job with his former employers.

Needless to say, I was slightly baffled. Tom had to work his way around so many unnecessary hurdles when eliminating many of those hurdles involved simply investing in the business. Too often the small business owner sees that expensive fix on a piece of equipment as money out of their personal pocket instead of an investment in the business for better performance. Yes, it is the same pocket it is coming out of, but the attitude of trying to keep the money in owner's personal pocket is detrimental to a business.

As I listened to Tom talk about his working conditions I was surprised he hadn't changed jobs more often! Showing up every day knowing you are going to have to use your MacGyver skills just to operate a piece of equipment so you can produce parts that are under deadline? Talk about unpredictable and stressful! For any employee, these situations would lead to wanting to find a new place to hang your hat. So much of Tom's history made sense, and I was thankful I didn't read too much into his resume and make the wrong assumptions.

As his interview wrapped up, we shared some pleasantries. I let Tom know that we would talk it over as a team and I would be in touch in the next few days. He made his way out the door and into the parking lot to head on his way. As he walked out, I knew one thing for sure: we were the right place for Tom. It may sound arrogant, but I just knew that our team and the 467 culture was the right place for him. Some of the things that were most important to him were already a part of the work environment we provided. He wanted emotional support, communication and the tools and resources needed to do his job. Not too much of a tall order, but something that had fallen short in his previous experiences.

My confidence level was extremely high that we were the right place for Tom, but the big question was … was Tom the right guy for us?

As he walked out to the parking lot, I was feeling fairly confident that Tom might be a pretty good fit for us. I wasn't 100 percent there, but rarely do I get to that point before we need to make a decision. I was speaking with some of the team members about Tom to gather their thoughts and impressions. As I turned around,

I was caught off guard. Tom was back in the building. As he walked toward me, he spoke words I will never forget: "I'm sorry to bother you, but could I have one more moment of your time?"

I was, of course, intrigued and asked him to continue. "As I was walking out to the parking lot, I said to myself, 'I just know this is a place that I would want to work.' I appreciate what you shared with me, and your parents seem like great people to work for as well. I love that this place is so clean, and that you invest in your people and equipment. If you would give me an opportunity to work here, I would bring a sleeping bag to store here, so if I ever needed to keep the machines running all night long to get a job out I would do it."

Home. Freaking. Run.

There it was. He was dead serious about working all night if needed. Of course, we didn't want that to happen, but wow, what an impression he made to me of the hunger he had become a part of this team. He was already "all in" and it wasn't even day one for him. What a humbling experience to have someone want to be on your team that badly. I of course explained we hoped that would never be needed, but appreciated his enthusiasm and level of interest. He let me know that was all he needed to add, and that he looked forward to hearing from us. Quite honestly, I almost hired him right on the spot, but doing so would have gone against our team decision process for new hires.

Eleven years later, Tom is still on our team. He isn't bouncing around from job to job like his resume would have suggested. We have managed to keep his sleeping bag at home, but I cannot count the number of times where Tom has stepped up to come in early, stay late, or sneak in on the weekend … you name it, whatever the job is, Tom is in. When you ask Tom for a favor, he says "whatever you need" before you are even done asking for what you want. And as you can imagine, that mentality and willingness to do anything for the team has rubbed off on the other team members who have joined in the years since Tom was hired.

Growing 467: Process

As our team grew, we modified our hiring processes. Our experience with Tom convinced us we needed to get better at learning more about the person who came to interview, not just their resume, during the interview process.

Each new team member needs to catch the vision, but also work well with the team. We knew that team chemistry and shared vision were going to trump experience and industry knowledge. However, in order to make sure we had found the right fit, my dad and I decided that we were not going to make new hire decisions based solely on our experience with the candidate. Hiring needed to involve group input so that we could make the right decision for the team.

Once we realized how important this decision would be, we revamped our entire interview process. As I have spent time with other FASTSIGNS centers and colleagues with small businesses in different industries, they have continually asked how we find such great people. I now realize that what we do, while simple, is not normal.

The first step in the process is to get the entire team on the same page to answer one simple question: "What are we looking for in our next team member?" We've had many of these conversations and have grown an understanding and respect for the core values we are looking for that will mesh well with our existing team. We want each new hire to make us all the better.

As we started to identify our new process, we came across a book that put everything we were looking for in a nice package that made it easier to communicate. Patrick Lencioni wrote *The Ideal Team Player: How to Recognize and Cultivate the Three Essential Virtues*, which is a book I recommend often.[1] If you haven't read it, I would strongly encourage you to set this book down for a second, go to your reading or listening style of choice and make the purchase. It's that good. I don't know Patrick, and I doubt that our paths will ever cross, so this is not some type of cross-promotional marketing. His book is just that good.

The premise of the book is about adapting your hiring practices to look for team members who are hungry, humble, and smart. While the ideas behind "hungry" and "humble" are pretty self-explanatory, the "smart" Lencioni refers to is related more to emotional intelligence than intellectual intelligence. While his book explained what we were already practicing, the way he broke it down in three simple terms made sense to me.

I naturally gravitated toward this book's content and then shared it with a few members of our team to read. The team bought into the concept, and we now have a stake in the ground that defines what we are looking for in simple terms when we interview future candidates. (Side note: having the entire team understand the importance of hungry, humble, and smart also helps professional development plans for current team members as it is rare that someone is performing perfectly in all three categories.)

---

1 Jossey-Bass Publishers, 2016, ISBN 9781119209591

Growing 467: Practice

The first step is to make sure the entire team understands what we are looking for in any new hire. Check. Got it. Now, the next steps seem fairly simple, but are critical.

First, post a job. Sounds simple, right? But understand that when you're posting a job, it's ok to share why you love what you do! So when you write the job description, think about what you find exciting about coming to work every day. Why would someone want to join your team and be a part of something special? Paint the picture. Tell the story!

In our world, we get to partner with people in the community to visually improve their company culture; launch a new brand; promote a nonprofit organization that benefits the community; welcome home military members coming back from serving overseas; and creatively solve challenges within clients' budgets to help them get their message out to grow their business. That's exciting! That has purpose.

"Running wide-format equipment on various substrates. RIP Software and printer experience preferred. Illustrator knowledge preferred, but not required." Does that sound exciting? That's a job description. We aren't running a business that's looking for people to do "a job"; we're running a business that's looking for people that want to join a team that's striving together to be better tomorrow than they were today. So, if we aren't hiring for "a job," then we shouldn't post "a job." We should post what we're really hiring for, and passion is allowed in a job description!

Okay, so now we have a job description that's designed to communicate energy and enthusiasm. Now that the job is posted, all we have to do is sit and wait for the applications to come in, right? Wrong! If you have a good platform to post your position, there should be a way for qualified applicants to find a link to the job posting. But step two in the process is sitting down and listing out all of the people in your sphere of influence who you would trust to refer someone to you to join your team. Customers, suppliers, friends, family, church members, friends from the gym—it doesn't matter where they come from, they just need to meet two simple criteria: First, do you trust them to refer the right type of person you need for your business, and second (and most important), do they know you and your business well enough to truly know what you are looking for in a team member? This is just as important as trusting them to refer to a quality individual to you.

Many people in my circle of influence have heard me talk about the "hungry, humble and smart" philosophy that Lencioni promotes. They also understand our culture and our business, so they know what we are looking for as a fit for new team members. They also know me personally and understand our company's values and goals.

Perhaps you are looking at your business and you don't like the culture that exists. Maybe that's why you are reading this book. That's ok! I would encourage you to have conversations within your circle of influence and paint the picture of the culture you want to build into your business. It's ok to let others know that you aren't happy with your current culture. Sometimes we let pride get in the way of a good authentic conversation, and the better the people you surround yourself with know the path you are trying to take with your business, the more likely they are going to be able to help guide the right people your way.

Back to the issue at hand. You've posted your job and fired up the pipeline of influencers who can guide people to the posting. At this point, hopefully some applicants are starting to filter in from those referrals. One thing to note: If you get a referral from someone you trust, always, always give that applicant at least a phone interview. Even if you look at a person's resume and think there is no way they'll be a match, they still deserve the courtesy of a phone interview. A note of appreciation should also go to the contact who referred that person to you. It doesn't matter if they get hired or not; someone made the effort to send someone your way, so out of respect for both the applicant and the person who referred them, that potential candidate needs at least a phone interview.

As you work through the phone interviews, I encourage you to keep them short and sweet. Ten minutes is all that is typically needed. The goal is to get a feel for the person, hit some of the key questions and help formulate an idea of how "hungry, humble and smart" apply to the individual. Some good questions include, "How have you resolved a conflict in the workplace?" "Talk about a time you took on a project and had to go above and beyond to make it a great success." "What have you learned from a coworker that you will always remember?" These three questions alone—resolving conflict (smart), going above and beyond (hungry), and learning from a coworker (humble)—are simple ways to start to identify these areas of interest.

There are many ways to filter the list of phone interviews down, but I try to move away from people who talk on and on about themselves and have not taken the time to learn about our business.

The next step is an in-person interview. Again, nothing earth-shattering here. However, we have found great value in conducting the interview along with someone on the team who could potentially be working closely with this person, and it doesn't always have to be a supervisor. At this point, we have established that team chemistry is important, so our thought is, why wait? Testing out some of the team chemistry to find the right fit can happen during this first in-person interview.

We also find it very helpful to give the candidate a tour of the facility and introduce them to other potential team members. We communicate to our team when we have interviews, so they always know and can anticipate meeting and saying hello to potential new hires. While these conversations rarely go beyond simple pleasantries, it is important for the candidate to see your operation and get a feel for some of the people on the team.

After interviewing a handful of candidates, it is good to review the individuals and their interviews with some of your team members, not just the other person or people who were in the interview. This gives the team a chance to ask questions about each candidate and dig a little deeper so that you can collectively identify the best candidates out of the applicant pool. That helps team buy-in when trying to determine who the team wants to bring in for the last stage of the interview process.

The last stage of the interview process is a half-day interview. This is where our process breaks the mold of what's typical. First, the candidate joins our morning meeting at 8:00 sharp. For the next fifteen minutes they will be lost, confused, and slightly overwhelmed at the amount of information that gets communicated between departments in a 15-minute period. The point isn't to overwhelm the candidate, it is to show them how we are all interdependent and need to work as a team. We need to start the day together!

As our prepress operator calls out "break," the team scatters and starts their day. The next four hours of the candidate's time with us will be four of the fastest hours of his or her life. Prior to the candidate's arrival, a schedule has been shared internally so the entire team is on the same page for the next four hours. The candidate gets shuffled from one person to the next with one key objective: to help the candidate see how each person takes responsibility within his or her role. It is important to know how things operate and get a picture of what we really do; however, even more important, the candidate and the team member get a chance to get to know each other. And while they do, can you guess what that team member is looking for? You got it: Hungry. Humble. Smart.

Establishing the "Why"

Now, I need to hit pause for a moment on the interview process. Before I take you through the end of it, I want to pause and truly establish the "why" behind our process. Too often I see interviewing candidates as a one-way process. After an employer posts a "job," they make multiple cuts in the interview process, finally presenting the best candidate with the job offer. This can be perceived as a very one-sided relationship, as if the employer carries the power and is so kind and generous to offer the job to the candidate. Sometimes it almost feels as if the employer is handing out a prize or a trophy: "Congratulations, you're the winner!"

There are multiple issues with this type of relationship between potential employer and candidate. And unfortunately, the example I am going to use to illustrate this is terribly embarrassing, but hang in there with me.

First off, if I had a man card left, this is when I would turn it in, but since I am sure it has been revoked so many times already, I will assume I don't need to continue with that formality. So, there are these two television shows, *The Bachelor* and *The Bachelorette*. I wish I could say I had never seen these shows before, but that would be a lie. I also wish I could just blame it on my wife for watching these shows when I just happened to be in the room, but that also would be a lie. While the number of episodes I have seen is quite low, I have definitely sat and watched. Now, maybe you love the show, or perhaps you just passed some serious, and perhaps well-deserved, judgment on me.

But in all seriousness, I'm convinced that the desire of the girls trying to "win" the bachelor or the guys trying to "win" the bachelorette causes the individuals vying for the stars' attention to lose sight of what they are really doing. Their focus is so locked in on winning that what happens after the person "wins" pales in comparison to winning the show. The contestants who are trying to win the heart of the bachelor or bachelorette want to beat out the competition. What's more, they don't want to be told by the star of the show that they didn't win! The fear of being rejected by the bachelor or bachelorette can drive contestants to fear losing more than wanting to win. What really confuses me are guys or girls who are totally heartbroken after not receiving a rose a couple of days into the show. Are you kidding me? Did they truly see a future with that bachelor or bachelorette, or are they just crushed that they lost?

Hopefully you are getting my point. Ask yourself, as an employer, are you creating a job to win, or an opportunity for someone to join the team and be a part of something special? While your intentions may be the latter, make sure your actions support your goals.

When we interview candidates, we make it very clear that this is not a one-way interview. We see this as an opportunity for each candidate to interview us as well. We refuse to sugarcoat areas in our business that need work, or dangle out carrots to tempt good candidates to commit. We will be transparent and will air our dirty laundry in addition to explaining some of the great things about what we do and who we are.

Yes, we want to talk to candidates who really want to "win" the job, but even more we want candidates who are looking ahead to the months and years after they say, "I do." We want them to truly experience who we are and understand what it means when we say that at 467, we are a family business that puts "We Before Me." This isn't just a bullet point on a presentation given by the president or a hiring manager; it is experienced as the candidate interacts with others on the team.

The interview process is not just an investment by our team; it is an investment by the candidate. We are fortunate that someone would be willing to spend a half day with us, and the candidate is fortunate that an organization they are interested in will open their doors to let them get a true feel for the organization before making a decision. Neither party should feel like they are doing the other a big favor; rather, this experience is intended to be a partnership. We show respect for that time by sending a pre-offer letter (contingent on the results of the interview) prior to the half-day interview. This allows the candidate to ask any questions about pay, vacation, benefits, retirement plans, and the like. We would never want to be in a spot where both parties invested their valuable time only to find that the goals in these areas did not align, and both parties wasted a half day doing due diligence on a partnership that would never come to fruition.

The Final Steps of the Process

Unpause. Let's get back to the process.

As you can imagine, in this half-day interview the candidate spends time with all of the team members. In each area he or she learns more about the process and the philosophies behind 467, and gets to know the people they may get to call coworkers in the near future. This continues until lunch is brought in for the entire team.

At that point we all gather around the table, just like we did four hours prior at our morning meeting. This is one of my favorite moments of the process, as I get to see some of the interactions taking place as people are gathering. In four short hours, this individual got to know our team members. And while everyone had a chance to ask some questions, there are still more questions to ask. Standing around the table, we will go around and each person will ask one more question. While it may be intimidating for a candidate to answer each question with everyone looking at them, it works really well. Our team continues to ask great questions and it always makes me proud when I can see the question pointing right back at the three critical areas we evaluate: humble, hungry and smart.

At that point I will spend some time with the candidate before they leave asking one simple question: "So, how did it go?" Without fail, one of the many comments I receive is, "This was great. I have never participated in something like this before, and it was really helpful." When I hear that I know we fulfilled our commitment to make this a two-way street. We gave the candidate a true opportunity to ask questions to each person, to see the process, and to really get a chance to envision what it might look like if they joined the team.

As I escort them to the door to thank them for their time, I let them know the last part of the interview: I will talk to each individual team member as well as the team as a whole, and we are looking for a unanimous "thumbs up" to send out the official offer letter.

Wow. Unanimous? Yes, unanimous. The team knows that once the candidate makes their way to the parking lot, they can expect to see me walking around making the gesture of "thumbs up," "thumb sideways," and "thumbs down." It's my way of asking, what do you think? If there is not an agreement, we talk about it. We go over the team's concerns. We take those concerns and see how they relate to hungry, humble and smart. If we aren't in agreement, we don't make the offer. If we are all in agreement, we will extend the offer.

Now this is where it gets really fun for me: when we extend the offer. It's at this point where we created something extremely special in our process. We make sure we're trying to walk in the shoes of the person receiving the offer letter. When they get that letter, they know that everyone they spent time with wants them to be on their team. Since they are privy to the process and know that we need everyone on board in order to extend the offer, in getting that letter they get their first affirmation as part of our team. When they walk in on their first day of work there are two things they know for sure: First, everyone wants them to be there; second, they know the people they will be working with. So their first day of orientation doesn't involve going around and meeting people and learning what they do. We already covered that!

But that isn't even the best part. Many times we are bringing in team members who don't have industry experience or experience in the types of skills they will be using. In order to be successful, they are going to need help. It will take a team effort to get the person trained, up to speed, and to be there when they have questions. In addition, everyone makes mistakes. After all, our veteran team members of 10+ years make mistakes. So what are the chances the new team member makes mistakes? 100 percent. It will happen. It will cost the company money when it does. And the new team member might even make the same mistake twice. Guess what? That's ok. We have a full team of people who said, yes, we want them on our team. They have adopted this person into the family. With that they are taking responsibility to help this person grow and develop and to be successful.

Have you ever been hired for a job and on your first day, you meet the people you are going to be working with? Or on your first day, you learn how your role impacts other roles within the company to truly get a bigger picture of what you will be doing? After developing this process, it makes me cringe to think people experience that type of first day. And yes, maybe your company has hundreds of team members, or team members in multiple locations, but hopefully the concept is not lost. Collaboration is critical to success.

Remember what Catherine Monson said when introducing 467 as a top five center in the network? "They get so much more than the sum of the individual parts." That is collaboration. That doesn't start once someone is brought on board; it starts before the job offer is even made. When someone has a say in the decision, they are naturally more invested in the decision that was made. Our team does not have the luxury of saying, "Ugh, why did 'he/they' hire that guy? He is never going to work out." It is not "he/they" who have made the decision; it is *we*. We hired that person, and we are going to fight like crazy to collectively get them up to speed as soon as we can.

The process above is simple, but it takes effort. It takes time. It takes communication. But if done well, and done as a team, the best hire is made.

This process is most difficult when you have an immediate need that you want to fill ASAP. It is easy to want to skip steps in the process, to just go from the in-person interview to an offer and skip the half-day process. After all, the candidate has to schedule time away from their current job if they are still working. And if you're in that much of a rush to hire someone, that probably means that you don't have a team full of people standing around wondering if there is anything to do that day.

Most likely the sense of urgency is because help is needed and the idea of people spending time during the interview process with the candidate could slow them down from the pile of work they already have to do. My biggest advice in those times is "trust the process." Stick with it. Yes it is a lot, and yes it takes time. However, don't look how the half-day interview will impact the next few weeks or months. Look further out. The better the decision you make, especially when you give the candidate the opportunity to make the best decision for them, creates a better probability of their being an effective part of the team in the long term.

So. . . you did it. You made the right hire. You have a great team member who is collaborating well with the team. Now. . . how do you keep them?

CHAPTER 6
"HE JUST MAKES SIGNS"

NICK CONTINUED TO GROW within his passion of gloving. Now, before you flip to the back of this book to see if there is a glossary, or Google search "gloving," let me make it a little bit easier on you and give you the quick description. Gloving is an activity/art/expression that is performed by wearing gloves with lights on the fingertips. Glovers will put on shows for individuals, large groups, or just themselves. Glovers typically perform in a darker environment to give the lights a more vibrant effect. Now, if I tried to go into more detail on all of the elements of this art/craft/hobby, I would not do it the justice it deserves.

Gloving is very common at music festivals and raves. Nick has developed many great relationships through this community. He's even started a new community of his own that he and his friends called TNL, or Thursday Night Lights.

While there are a wide range of friendships developed within this community, Nick would say that common characteristics of these friends are that they are introspective, thought provoking, and passionate people. There are a large variety of passions within this group of Nick's friends that range from protecting the environment, to fostering positive self-worth, to making creative apparel, to supporting human rights and respecting the need for and promoting quality mental health services. As they interact, Nick can challenge his friends with some thought-provoking questions, and they can do the same to him.

One evening, one of his close friends asked him a simple but extremely powerful question: "Why do you *just* make signs?"

Wow. In one simple question, Nick was feeling challenged about the purpose of his work life. This one simple question invoked a full range of emotions. First, he was angry. Why would this so-called friend disrespect his line of work? He felt misunderstood and disappointed that a close friend didn't really appreciate the work he performed and the things he made. Next, he felt challenged. What if his friend was right? What if all his career involved was just printing some signs and that was it, period? At the time he had just celebrated his sixth year with us; had he just wasted six years of his life? What was he contributing to society more than just hitting the print button throughout the day? This one single question really set Nick into a deep, thought-provoking and self-reflective period of his life.

While this was a challenging, frustrating and at times depressing question for Nick to ponder, I couldn't have been happier that he'd been asked the question. You may wonder why. Why would I want someone to challenge Nick in a way that might cause him to leave our team in search of something more fulfilling? Why would I want to risk losing a talented team member with years of experience? Why would I want to put our team in a position where we might have to start recruiting to replace someone who was fully trained and extremely productive?

The answer is simple. In fact, I may have to get a little wild here and go so far to say, the answer to that question is *so stinking simple.* If Nick truly felt like he was just printing signs and that was his purpose at work, I had failed. We had failed. And if we've somehow failed a valued team member, I want to know why.

Creating Purpose

This question, coming from outside of our business, gave us a chance to hit the pause button and reflect on how we are creating purpose. Nick's professional development, his purpose, his contribution, and his ability to influence a community are very evident within our team. These aspects of Nick's purpose as a team member have been developing as a continuous process from the time he was hired, and will continue to be developed as part of his professional growth process. However, if helping Nick understand his value was not a priority within our culture and we decided to start trying to figure out what Nick's contribution and purpose was within the team after he'd been asked this difficult question, he would be long gone.

Quite honestly, if Nick were just a printer operator, with all of the passion, creativity and positive energy he has, I would hope he would leave. He is too talented of a human being to be defined by a single task. But as you can imagine from the previous chapter where we talked about finding hungry, humble and smart team members, those three descriptors apply both to Nick and to our entire team.

If you have someone in your organization who has a singular purpose to perform a task, one of two things is happening: Either you are looking at the person and underestimating and underutilizing their potential, or you are not clearly communicating how his role is important for the team. If neither of these are true, then you have the wrong person on the team, or you don't need to fill the role.

You may be thinking, "Whoa… wait a minute Mike, I think you are going a little overboard, aren't you? I mean, come on, what about the guy who just picks up the trash throughout the plant? Literally, that is his job. He picks up scrap materials and trash and gets rid of them. That's all he does. His purpose is just picking up trash, period. Right?"

Wrong! Without even stepping foot into your facility, I would bet that is not the case. In fact, if you think you have someone in your organization who has a singular purpose of simply performing a task, email me. I want to know what it is, because I'm convinced that such a job doesn't exist. But before you fire off that email, let's think about the guy who "just picks up trash."

How important is it for your team to work in a clean environment? If he wasn't picking up trash or scraps, who would do it? Would it be the machine operators? If so, would that take away from their efficiencies of producing products? And what about the scrap or trash that ends up on the floor: Does that create a safety concern? Do you ever bring current or prospective customers through your facility for tours? If so, how important is it that you have a clean environment? Do you have team members that appreciate working in a clean environment, and take pride in a clean workspace? Do you recycle, and if so, does it require some sorting when the trash or scraps are collected?

If you ask me, we just asked some questions that illustrate why the guy picking up trash is an important part of the company, as he deals with all kinds of critical areas: production, safety, sales, company culture and protecting the environment.

Still you might say, "Ok, Mike... that is a little bit of a stretch, isn't it?" Here is my quick answer: No. No, it isn't. Why do we get so wrapped up in the task we need completed instead of seeing how important the person behind the task is? Why do we minimize how integral they are to the production process and team functioning? You may think, "Since I could probably find anyone to come in and pick up trash and scraps, it must not be that important of a position." Wrong again. We just outlined the importance of the role, and just because the skill set does not require a master's degree, that doesn't mean it is not of value!

Most importantly, the person behind the task is valuable. Making sure they understand their value and their impact on the company at large is critical to motivating them and the rest of the team to do their best work.

There may be many of you reading this that think I am a little crazy to make this big of a deal over a guy picking up trash. And for those of you who think that way, hold on, you are about to think I am even crazier.

Take the position of an engineer who is designing a new product that is going to be mass produced. If he makes a mistake, it could cost the company a significant amount of money and, depending on the product, may even create a liability issue if the product fails. Therefore, we can say the engineer is more valuable than the person picking up the trash, correct? Incorrect. Flat out wrong. I couldn't disagree more. Now, if you would rephrase it to say the task and responsibility of the engineer is more critical than the task of the person collecting trash, I agree. 100 percent correct.

The issue in all this is that we have somewhere in our society transferred how critical the task is to the value of the human being who is performing the task. Yes, the engineer is a very valuable human being, but so is the person picking up the trash. Both positions deserve respect, appreciation, constructive feedback, evaluations from peers, and goals for growth and development.

"Wait, now you want a growth and development plan for the person picking up trash?" Yes. Absolutely. Is there a more efficient way to handle the trash? Could he be cross-trained in other areas, so on lighter trash days he can help other team members out in different areas? Can he track the scrap that's being tossed that might have been able to be reused or converted into a product?

Yes, he can be challenged. Yes, he can be held accountable. So yes, he can have a growth and development plan.

Nick's Journey at 467

Now let's circle back to Nick. I want to reiterate that if we had waited to work with Nick to make sure he understood his purpose and value until after he was asked the question, "Why do you *just* make signs?", we would have lost him. And if that had been the case, our organization would have been classified as normal. Sad, but true. Unfortunately, it is all too common for people to feel undervalued or feel like they have only one singular purpose within their work environment. Instead of writing in generalities, I want to get more specific about Nick and his journey.

We were on the hunt to find the next member of our production team. Through our supplier network, we heard there was this young "kid" working in a sign shop a couple hours north of us who was going to be getting married and moving back to Grand Rapids. While I typically cringe when someone refers to a team member as a "kid," it probably is a fairly accurate depiction of who Nick was at the time. He joined our team in 2013 as a 20-year-old with so much to learn. The best part of all this is that I could tell early on he was up for the journey.

When he hired on, Nick was feeling valued and important early on in his career with us. That's a simple statement, but why did he feel this way? A big reason he felt that way is that he had a voice, and we listened. If he had an idea, we wanted to hear it. If he thought we could try to do something in a different way, we talked about it with an open mind.

Unfortunately, just listening is a little too uncommon in many work environments, but the next step is even more uncommon: We helped to implement his ideas! It sounds simple, but too often team members come up with ideas that management believes are good, but then they sit on the back burner and don't get implemented. For a team member to know that his idea was heard makes that person feel important. But for management to take those ideas and implement them, that's a different level all together. They get to see firsthand the value they are bringing to the team.

Another area where Nick felt valued and important came from two simple little words strung together that he heard frequently: "Thank you." We appreciated his efforts; we appreciated his willingness to learn; we appreciated his willingness to stay a little late if needed to make sure a project was completed. So... we thanked him.

It almost seems silly to write about those two words, but they matter. I once had a conversation with an owner of a small business who mentioned that he had an employee who was really, really good. He was a newer employee, but he was doing a great job. I asked him how he let this employee know he was doing a great job, as I am always curious about how others recognize this behavior in their organizations. His response blew my mind. "I don't really do anything. I'm afraid that if I let him know how great he is, he'll ask me for more money." Since this is a PG-rated book, I won't share the exact thoughts I had when I heard this come out of his mouth, but the edited version is "You're an idiot."

Why is it that so many managers or owners assume the only way team members will feel valued is through monetary compensation? This is a rhetorical, open-ended question without an answer because I cannot figure it out. Most would prefer to not admit this is how they think, but their behaviors and policies say differently. Now, I'm not saying there are not people out there who only feel valued by the number on their check stub every two weeks, but I really think such people are an extreme minority. Quite frankly, why would you want that type of person in your organization anyway? A person who is motivated solely by compensation is demonstrating a "Me Before We" mentality—the opposite of what we do our best to promote at 467.

All that said, it is important to know that over the last ten years, Nick has been on a great financial growth journey. He has received raises that exceeded his expectations, monthly bonuses based on the team achieving their goals, and year-end bonuses that were above and beyond what he could have imagined. He has received raises and bonuses that have been more than what we needed to give to "keep him." But our goal isn't to just keep Nick, it is to partner with him in his personal, professional and financial growth journey. So I am not trying to suggest that finances can be kicked to the side, but too often when we make this the focal point of an employer/employee relationship, we miss the mark.

Hopefully by now you're getting the picture: Nick was feeling appreciated; he was sharing his ideas and they were being heard. As he continued to learn, we gave him more and more responsibilities to take on and empowered him to make his own decisions about process and products. When it came time to purchase an extremely expensive piece of printing equipment, his was a key voice in the decision-making process. When it arrived, we gave him the keys to the printer and let him know it was his baby. He was even given the responsibility of naming the printer (we have creative names for our equipment). He couldn't have been more excited to take on these responsibilities, and every once in a while he had to pinch himself to think that our team trusted him with so much.

His development continued in learning that piece of printing equipment, and he grew from being the operator of the machine to becoming a true technician. Any maintenance, service or decisions that needed to be made about the printer, Nick was the guy. He began to thrive, and continues to thrive in terms of being a true master of producing great products on that piece of equipment. As a small business owner, I naturally have a lot to worry about, but managing the performance of Nick's printer and that process isn't one of them. He has it under control and he successfully cross-trains other team members so that when he's not there, I still have no worries.

If that was the essence of Nick's journey, you might say it is a success story. I wouldn't disagree. He is an engaged team member who takes on responsibility and ownership, continues to find ways to improve the process and quality, and goes above and beyond in educating himself on the equipment so that he's able to service the equipment or partner with the service technician from the manufacturer when the printer needs repair. Not too bad for a then-20-year-old "kid" who walked through our doors in 2013. But that isn't even the best part of Nick's growth. The hard skills, the cross-training, the product and technical knowledge are critical to our business and executing projects well. However, the soft skills of leadership development are what foster an environment of team growth and development.

When Nick came through our doors he wasn't the strongest in team member communication. He struggled with conflict resolution; he brought with him a short temper; he brought a fear of "messing up"; and he brought a perception of what a manager/employee relationship looked like. As you can imagine, we learned most of this through experiencing it with Nick. He didn't show up on day one and explain all of his shortfalls. However, we don't mind shortfalls, as we see those as opportunities for individuals to grow.

Slowly but surely we began sharing leadership training for Nick (and the whole team). We used internal and external resources, but we really made these topics a part of our communication and culture. We didn't send Nick to a seminar to go "get fixed" and then expect him to come back as a very patient person that handled conflict and its resolution like a pro. At the time of this writing, Nick still struggles at times in a couple of these areas, and completely thrives in others. But today he handles the areas he struggles with so much more effectively than in years past. And he is so much more self-reflective than ever before. Regardless of the situation, he knows he needs to start with the phrase we use frequently: "My Response is My Responsibility." No matter what the circumstances are that come his way, he knows he needs to take full responsibility for the way he reacts.

So, how does this impact our business? Nick is viewed as a leader, a listener, and a contributor, and he brings with him an infectiously positive energy. He approaches every day as an opportunity to make it an awesome day, and he makes sure that his team members know how awesome he thinks they are... every... day.

But these soft skills of leadership go far beyond the walls of our business. Within his Thursday Night Lights gloving community, he has taken many of the leadership skills he's learned at FAST-SIGNS 467 and applied them to this group. His ability to have better conflict resolution with friends has reached an entirely new level. He's been able to take the feeling we give him of being empowered and transfer it to others in his gloving community. When faced with a tough situation, he thinks about how I or someone on our team might handle it.

For nearly ten years now, Nick has lived in our business seeing examples of how our training and conversation about building soft skills in interpersonal situations works. Now he is applying those learned skills outside of work. But these skills don't just apply to Nick's participation in the gloving community. As a husband and a father of two, he is applying these same skills to become a better family man.

Rest assured that we don't take the credit for Nick's growth and development. Nick's growth has been up to him. We cannot make someone else grow personally and professionally. However, we do take some credit for creating the environment and investing time and energy into Nick to provide him the opportunity to grow personally and professionally.

From the beginning, Nick was "all in"; he humbled himself to be open to growth and improvement, and every day he strives to be the best version of himself that he can possibly be. So, after ten years we have someone on our team who is a leader, who is a positive influence on our entire team, who is creatively using his passions inside and outside of work, who is supporting others' ideas, and who is making sure that his team knows he is always there to support them with their workload.

Nick is better developed to make a bigger impact in our business, but also in the lives of those outside of work. He is helping positively change the lives of other people. And the best part is, his growth journey is far from over. He wants to continue to grow professionally and personally and is working toward doing so consistently. He has failed in some attempts, and that's ok. He picks himself back up, or if needed, we pick him back up and we'll both try again.

I think if the 20-year-old Nick walked through our doors today, the 30-year-old Nick probably wouldn't even recognize him. If you ask me, that's a pretty amazing journey for a guy who *"just makes signs."*

CHAPTER 7

"IS THIS SEAT TAKEN?"

TIM HAD BEEN WITH OUR TEAM for five years. He spent the first couple of years as a member of our inside sales team, and then after some personnel changes, we had an opening for an outside sales team member that we thought Tim might want to consider.

After five years of sales, Tim had developed some great relationships, successfully led the charge on some creative and innovative projects, and continued to grow and learn with our ever-changing industry. Not only did he develop great relationships with the customers, but he also had great relationships with our team members. So, if you took a glance from the outside, you would probably confirm that we had a pretty good thing going with Tim in that role. Great for Tim. Great for FASTSIGNS. A win/win situation, right? Not exactly.

It was at the four-year mark that Tim approached me in a pretty vulnerable moment. As he held back some tears, he explained to me that he wasn't happy. He wasn't enjoying the work anymore. What used to be a joyful drive into work to pull into the parking lot had started to turn into a drive that he dreaded as he knew he would have to face whatever challenges were waiting for him as he walked through the doors. At one point, Tim had viewed customer challenges as an opportunity to deliver a creative solution that would exceed the customer's expectation. That feeling had eroded to the point that Tim now saw customer challenges as an opportunity for something to go wrong. A customer expressing any type of frustration, regardless of whether we had any control over resolving the customer's frustration, now felt personal to Tim.

Tim was no longer enjoying what he was doing, but he had a dilemma. He absolutely loved FASTSIGNS. He found the product to be interesting and innovative; he loved how our business was connected to the community in providing signs and graphics to household names of our community; and most importantly, he loved the team. The thought of trying to find another line of work and leaving the team did not sound appealing to Tim. The thought of staying with the team he loved but being unhappy in his role didn't sound appealing either.

Just a note before I continue: It's important for you to know that Tim never really wanted to have a career in sales. It just happened that he was interested in our organization and that the inside sales position that was open. He ended up doing well in sales, but it was the product and the team that fueled his passion, not the role he was in. He got the hang of it, and many times he really enjoyed what he was doing, but that feeling ended up wearing off. So, now what?

Listen and Learn

The next step for me in this situation was pretty simple: Listen. Ask some questions, let Tim talk, and patiently listen to what he had to say. I asked him, what interested him? What would make him feel fulfilled in the work he was doing? How could he use his talents and skill set in a way that would make the drive into the parking lot feel better?

At this point in the process my goal was simply to seek to understand. These were challenging questions for Tim to answer, and he didn't have, or need to have, the answers right on the spot. There was a lot of self-reflection that Tim needed to do, and I wanted to give him the time and space to do this.

As I asked these questions and listened, Tim knew that I was on his side to help him navigate this difficult time in his professional career. I wasn't going to try and convince him that everything was fine and that this was just a phase he was going through. I wasn't going to dismiss his feelings. But I also wasn't going to hold back and not challenge him to dig deep and really figure out the root causes of his unhappiness.

Tim worked through his thoughts and came back to me. When he did, he told me that he wanted to continue to be a part of the dynamic FASTSIGNS team, but that rather than staying in inside or going to outside sales (which can be a lonely world to live in), he really wanted to work with his hands. Gaining this clarity led him to understand his desire to join our production team.

I strongly believe that it is important not only to have great team members, but also make sure they are in the right position. We often refer to the book *Good to Great: Why Some Businesses*

Make the Leap and Others Don't by Jim Collins.[2] He illustrates the concept of making sure organizations have "the right people on the bus," and then ensuring that "the right people are in the right seats." There was no doubt that Tim was the right person to have on our bus, but it appeared that he hadn't been sitting in the right seat for a while.

As a small business with fewer than twenty people on the team, we had a problem. The seat Tim could fill and fill well as a member of the production team was taken. We had a talented production team, so we didn't have any need to move someone off the bus and upgrade a position. We were staffed appropriately, so adding an additional team member did not make sense financially for the business. We were stuck, but we needed an action plan. Tim and I both had the same goal of him staying with the FASTSIGNS team. We also shared a goal of Tim feeling fulfilled at work and enjoying that drive into the parking lot. We needed a solution, but we didn't have one that could make that happen immediately.

Over the next fourteen months, Tim and I worked on finding a solution together. Wow, fourteen months! During that time we met weekly, with a few key objectives each and every week. The stress of the sales role was one of the main drivers causing Tim's lack of joy at work. My mission was to understand all of his stress points and look for opportunities to help reduce their effect. How could I support Tim as he solved challenging issues, worked through unfortunate situations, or just simply dealt with some customers who were less than pleasant? Those were the topics we discussed at length.

---

[2] HarperBusiness, 2001, ISBN 978066620992

My commitment was to support Tim in every way I possibly could, and Tim's commitment was to hang in there and continue to support his customers and our team to the best of his ability. A key factor that gave him hope was that I stuck with him, so he didn't feel like he was on this journey alone.

Now, don't get me wrong. There were some rough moments in those fourteen months, but through the growth of our business, we finally decided we needed to bring another person on board to join our production team. The time and energy Tim and I put into this situation was well worth it. When we brought Tim over to the production team, we knew that we had someone who was hungry, humble and smart. We knew that Tim could help elevate our production team.

We were also able to find a salesperson to join our team, more importantly we used this job switch as an opportunity to give other sales team members more responsibilities. In their new roles, they began to thrive and feel more empowered and valued as they took on bigger projects and larger accounts.

So here's the bottom line: Both our production team and sales team got stronger. Tim enjoys the work he's doing, and when the inside sales team had an opportunity to step up, they did, and did it well.

Hang in There and Fight for the Team

Many team members and managers/owners would have simply given up on this journey long ago. They wouldn't have put in the effort, telling their employee "it is what it is" and not providing any hope for change. Why would we put in the effort; why would we go through fourteen months of struggle to work through this?

This is where the value of our "467 culture" paid off. This was so much more than a decision to try and work it out. There were substantial factors that made the effort worth it.

From my perspective, I knew all along that Tim was someone we want on our bus. He had shown over his time with us that he was hungry, humble and smart. He not only caught the vision of 467 being more than just a sign company, but he also wanted to be a leader in this vision, not just a participant. He cared deeply for the other team members and wanted to support them, hold them accountable, and find ways to make sure they were being fulfilled in their work. He was willing to take direct feedback and look in the mirror and figure out how he could improve and get better. He was drinking the 467 Kool-Aid and it was tasting great, and he was making the place better because of it.

Tim was valuable and I greatly appreciated him on our team, and I wasn't alone. The entire team felt this way about Tim. So, does this sound like someone who is worth fighting for? Absolutely.

Now look at the situation from Tim's perspective. Tim felt encouraged, supported and listened to during all of his years on our team, not just when his role started to become less desirable. There was a history of support that he knew he could rely on through our actions, not just our words. He knew that we cared about him. He knew that when I said I would stick by his side and help him through this, I wasn't just giving him lip service. When he sat in my office with tears, telling me he felt like the world was crashing in on him, he knew there was no judgment coming from me.

When our discussions created opportunities for him to open up about his personal life and the challenges he was facing, he knew that each one mattered to me and that he could trust me with it.

We shared tears, hugs, and frustrations, but we were doing it together. When he was dealing with a customer who was irrational and rude and he was feeling all the stress in the world, he knew he could say, "Mike, I need help. Can you take this one?" Being a part of a team and company that would come alongside him like this was something he didn't want to give up. He loved it. He wanted to be a part of it. He was just in the wrong seat.

You may be thinking, "This sounds great, but it sounds like a lot of time, effort and energy on your end." Absolutely. It took a ton of time and effort. When you walk alongside someone who is in a darker place, it's difficult not to carry some of the emotional burden. Our one-on-one meetings each week far exceeded the planned fifteen to thirty minutes.

So, was it a lot of work? No, it was more than a lot of work. Was it exhausting when the next move or step was not clear, and I wasn't sure how I was going to be able to help Tim get in the right seat on the bus? Extremely. Did Tim ever know how difficult it was for me to navigate this situation and the burden I felt like I was carrying trying to help him through this? I'm not sure, but I hope not.

I don't need to be awarded a badge of honor for walking through the trenches with a team member; that's just part of the mission of "We Before Me." If I was only worried about my role and my responsibilities, I could have easily said I didn't have time to help Tim through this challenge. Tim was not an item on my checklist to get done; he was a valuable person going through a difficult time, and no matter how much that drive into work was something he was going to dread, there was one thing he knew for sure, the guy in the office on the other side of the wall from him had his back. I made sure he would never doubt that.

Bending over Backward

In Chapter 3 we talked about treating team members like customers. We bend over backward for customers, but when the time comes, whatever the situation looks like, are we ready to bend over backward for a team member?

There is no doubt that all of my efforts with Tim were good for the business. As we observed before, the production team got stronger, and the sales team had team members grow professionally to fill the gap when Tim transitioned. There is no question at the end of it all, our business is stronger and better because of this transition.

All this to say that if your focus is improving your business, taking the time to walkthrough the trenches with a team member is worth it. It will help your business. Even if the result does not turn out to be a favorable outcome, if your team members know you're willing to go through the trenches with them, you'll find opportunities to improve your business together. Not only was it my responsibility, it was also my privilege to work through this for Tim's benefit, but also for his family's benefit.

Tears come to my eyes as I type this just knowing how blessed I am to have opportunities to work with team members as someone they can count on to help create a better tomorrow. When you get to that point in your relationship with your team, the word fulfilling is an understatement.

Now, in the situation outlined with Tim, was it my responsibility to help create a better situation for him? Wasn't it up to Tim to figure that out? I mean after all, I am trying to lead a business. Who has time to spend hours and hours over months and months talking about how someone feels and whether or not they are happy? If you're in a similar situation and you have decided that as a leader in your business this kind of thing isn't your responsibility, I wouldn't argue with you. It's not necessarily your responsibility to help someone feel fulfilled in what they do and enjoy the drive into the parking lot each morning.

Is it a responsibility? No. Is it an opportunity? You bet! Leadership isn't about what you *have* to do, it is about what you *get* to do. I am forever grateful that Tim allowed me to join him on his journey. It led to a stronger FASTSIGNS team, a stronger Tim and an extremely grateful Michael. I would say that is worth the effort, wouldn't you?

Start Small

It can be overwhelming to try and connect with all of your team members, especially when you feel like your schedule is already overbooked. One way to get some momentum in this area is to keep it simple. Just simply ask a team member to tell you what was their win for the week? What went well? What are they proud of? You can follow that question by asking them to name something that was a struggle for them during the past week. What didn't go as planned? What could have gone better? Just asking about what went well and what didn't go so well can start a good conversation. And the answers don't always have to be about work!

What's important in all this is to follow these discussions by simply asking the question, "Is there anything I can do to better support you?"

Hopefully over time you will hear about successes, which you can then share with other team members. You will also hear about challenges your team has experienced and together you can look for opportunities to help overcome the obstacles. Your team will come to understand that when they ask you for help or support, they can trust you to follow through and show through your actions that you care.

While you are having these conversations to help support and coach your team, you will find that you learn a little more than you were expecting and receive more support than you had ever imagined.

CHAPTER 8

WHERE DID THE RAINBOWS AND UNICORNS GO?

WESLEY HAD BEEN WITH US for one year, which meant it was time for her annual review. In just her first year she brought in incredible sales numbers, the customers absolutely loved her, she was extremely efficient, her work ethic was unmatched, and her product knowledge continued to grow each and every day. In areas that were not as easy for her—mental math for example—she utilized tools and resources to improve her accuracy and efficiency. "Rock star" would be a great way to describe her performance.

Our review process includes getting feedback from all team members through a survey we send out prior to the anniversary date of the team member being reviewed. As I reviewed the information and spent some time discussing with the lead on the inside sales team, it was clear that Wesley needed to take the next steps in her professional growth. While she absolutely crushed her job in many ways and continued to improve and take on bigger projects, there were some areas that needed to be addressed to help the team dynamics and move her personal and professional growth forward.

Wesley has a big personality, and it's a good one. She is one of those people you can throw in the middle of a room where she doesn't know a soul, and she will walk out of that room an hour later with all kinds of new friends. In an open office environment, big personalities can present some challenges depending on the mix of personalities in the office. While that did play a little bit of a factor, the bigger factor was that the team felt that Wesley demonstrated an excessive amount of negativity and complaining that was draining the energy out of the rest of the team.

Wesley walked into my office for her annual review, and said, "Ok, don't make me cry." That was a simple ask, but I couldn't come through for her. There were tears, a lot of tears. Now, it's probably important to point out Wesley is not one who is prone to cry. No doubt that some of the team's feedback was very difficult for her to hear. As we went through her review together we celebrated the successes, but then we had a very direct conversation about her needing to take the next steps in her professional growth—reigning in her negative energy and not projecting that to the team. It wasn't an easy conversation, but it was needed.

Get Uncomfortable

Before we dive into the approach of the conversation, let's first recognize the normal response most managers and small business owners would take toward this conversation. One year in and this team member is crushing her goals, exceeding expectations, and customers love her. She also has the desire to increase her sales, take on more responsibility and is someone you can count on to get the job done. If asked to do something, you know it is going to be done. If your numbers are all good, what's the big deal if her big personality can come across as being negative sometimes? That's just Wesley, deal with it. We all have our quirks, that just happens to be hers. Let's just sweep the negativity under the rug because after all, a tiger can't change her stripes, right?

Most managers would figure, if I upset her, she might leave, or she might be so mad that she stops performing well. So instead of having the difficult conversation, they leave it alone

My suggestion? Get uncomfortable. Don't fall into the trap of sweeping a problem like this under the rug. Put the best interests of the team member and the team as a whole first, be prepared for what you're going to say, bite the bullet, and sit down to talk.

How does a manager have a productive conversation about something that they know someone is going to take personally? That is a loaded question, but an important one.

Kim Malone Scott wrote a fantastic book entitled, *Radical Candor: Be a Kickass Boss without Losing Your Humanity.*[3] I highly recommend reading the book, or at the very least viewing some of her YouTube videos as she explains the ideas behind Radical Candor. I will leave the detailed explanation to Kim, but the overarching message is to "care personally and challenge directly."

In her book, Scott tells a story of how, on a busy street corner, her dog was not listening to her. A man came up to her and said, "I can see you really love that dog." Right away he made a connection with her by recognizing and acknowledging her feelings toward her dog. She knew he cared personally from this statement. The next

---

[3] St. Martin's Press, 2017, ISBN 97812503505

words out his mouth were, "but you're going to kill this dog if you don't teach it how to sit."

He really had her attention at this point, and then he pointed at the sidewalk with a harsh gesture and said "Sit!" At his command, the dog sat. Scott didn't even know her dog could sit on command! She looked at this man in amazement. He then said, "It's not mean, it's clear." With that, he walked off, leaving her with words to live by—words we should all live by.

Caring and Confrontation

Going into this conversation, I knew it would be extremely important that Wesley knew I cared for her personally. First off, it's true, I do care personally for her. So as we started our conversation, I made sure she knew that she was appreciated and that I and the team were extremely fortunate to have her in our lives. I told her she is a very special person, and her decision to change careers and join our team was one I was extremely grateful for.

But following that, I didn't sugarcoat the impact her negativity was having on the team and why it needed to change. This was difficult for her to hear because she could have easily misinterpreted the information being given to her and think the team didn't want her around. This was far from the truth, but the feedback she was receiving was very personal. As we reviewed all the information together, there were some comments that she had a hard time understanding, and some comments made her feel she needed to defend herself. But overall she took the majority of the comments to heart and reflected on them.

It was a very tearful review. It was hard. It was exhausting. It was difficult to look across the table and see the sadness and hurt she was feeling from these comments. I managed to save my tears until after she left the room. Yes, I might be a little bit of a softy, but walking in her shoes and knowing how she was feeling in that moment, it was hard to keep my eyes completely dry. I knew that she was feeling defeated, frustrated and upset. But, without a shadow of a doubt, I also knew that she was confident she had my support. She knew I would be with her on this journey if she chose to take it. She knew that I would be there to give her a listening ear, a word of advice, and if needed a safe place to vent some of the negativity she was feeling instead of broadcasting it to the entire team.

Fast forward to today, and I'm happy to report that Wesley took the advice to heart and took action. She made changes, and the team noticed the difference in her work habits. She also elevated her professionalism across the board. Today she is more professional with her immediate team (sales) as well as with the design and production teams. While she has always maintained a level of professionalism with the clients she worked with, her talents in this area have grown and improved to a new level.

While I had personally observed all of these things, I also checked in with other team members to confirm what I was seeing. Unanimously, they all agreed. We made sure Wesley knew that her changes were noticed; she was encouraged and motivated to continue on the journey.

I couldn't be happier to see the personal growth and the positive steps she has taken in her professional growth; both are of great benefit to FASTSIGNS. However, caring enough to talk about these issues was bigger than that—it was great for Wesley as an individual.

While I'm hopeful I will have the opportunity for years and years to come to work with Wesley, I don't know where her interests and passions might take her. Regardless of where life takes her personally and professionally, she is now a better version of herself. She is more aware of how her negativity impacted others and she doesn't want to continue to create that type of environment for herself or others. Her team members were willing to provide feedback, and I made sure she could hear the feedback in a manner that was caring personally and professionally challenging. Through this process we created an opportunity for growth. The feedback wasn't mean, it was clear.

Follow the Process: Four Steps

In order for a manager to follow this approach, I recommend they follow four key areas to have the best chance of success.

Be Prepared

First and most important, be prepared. These kinds of conversations won't be successful if one just starts rambling without carefully planning out the conversation. After all, part of showing you care is putting the time and energy into making sure your words are going to be meaningful. If you know a conversation is going to be uncomfortable, rambling on and on won't help. Talking in circles will ensure you lose the impact of being clear and concise.

Remember that preparing for a conversation like this involves thinking about how you are delivering the information as well as how the person in question is going to receive the message. Messaging will need to be crafted differently depending on the personality and style of the team member. So take a minute to walk in their shoes. Remember, how the message is received is more important than how the message is given! Effective change when the person receiving the feedback is able to find a path forward and take action. Some people do better with paragraphs of explanation; others do better with bullet points. There isn't a right or a wrong way to frame this conversation, but the more it is crafted to how the person will best receive the information, the more effective the conversation will be, and the more likely it will lead to positive change.

Realize This is Just the Beginning

Second, understand that when the feedback is given, that represents the starting line, not the finish line. Many times managers will work hard to pull all of the feedback together, do their best to communicate it to the team member, and think their work is finished. Actually, the work in communication has just begun at that point. The feedback one is giving in the conversation invites the team member to start a new journey; but if you as a manager care personally for the welfare of your employee, realize that you've signed up to go on this journey as well. The journey may be as simple as checking in once a month, or it may involve more in-depth work on a weekly basis. You may need to dive a little deeper into situations that have been difficult for the team member in the past. No matter the situation, it is vitally important to make sure that in the review or in this conversation you don't just drop a bomb and then get out of Dodge.

Manage Your Expectations

Third, manage your expectations for change. I didn't expect Wesley to come in the following Monday all happy-go-lucky, not a care in the world and never breathing a word of a complaint again. First off, I don't think that kind of processing is healthy at any point in time, so as a manager, keep in mind most of these kinds of feedback loop cases will require a journey of change over time, not an immediate change. This will take patience and understanding on both of your parts as the team member takes steps to move in the right direction.

Of course, some types of feedback require immediate action; providing feedback that a team member needs to wear safety glasses is not worthy of a journey. In that case, immediate action and change is expected. But feedback that is behavioral and personal in nature doesn't typically engender change overnight, so be patient along the way and give the person a chance to grow on their journey.

Observe and Recognize the Changes

Finally, recognize the changes that are taking place. Even if they seem really small, if the changes are positive and seem to be moving in the right direction, let the person know you've noticed their hard work to make those changes. Not only does this kind of feedback motivate even more positive change, it also emphasizes your personal care for the team member and the situation. It reinforces that you are on the journey with them. And while there's a lot to be said about positively reinforcing changed behavior, you also have a responsibility to point out situations in which things haven't changed, or the change is not moving quickly enough.

While this chapter focused on Wesley's journey, I am happy to say we have plenty of stories like this that have ended positively. Providing feedback in this manner is something we at 467 strive for; it is an integral part of our culture. The value of giving and receiving feedback is understood, and we now have a team that welcomes feedback and puts a lot of thought into the type of feedback they give to others.

It was very encouraging to see our team integrate this type of culture. I will never forget the day I knew the team truly understood the power of feedback and how important it was. It was a nice fall day when Kristy walked into my office....

CHAPTER 9

UH OH . . . THERE'S A PROBLEM

KRISTY HAD PREVIOUSLY sent me a message asking if I could set aside some time so we could talk through some challenges the team was facing. Absolutely! My door is always wide open for conversations like that, and I was looking forward to hearing what Kristy had to share.

When she walked into my office, she didn't display her normal bubbly, upbeat demeanor. I could sense the conversation we were about to have was going to be a little more difficult than a typical conversation. Usually in those situations I pause and just keep telling myself to listen to what she has to say, try not to jump to conclusions, don't cut her off and defend the person or issue at hand, and by all means don't try and solve an issue before even hearing what it is.

She began explaining that the team felt like the culture was headed in the wrong direction. What's more, they were able to pinpoint a single source that was causing this issue. As I braced myself to hear which team member was causing the challenges, my mind started thinking through all of the next steps we would need to take to help get things back on track. Even though I reminded myself to just listen, there was no turning my brain off. I was already trying to solve a problem and I didn't even know what the problem was yet. Was it a conflict between sales and design? Sales and production? Installation and sales? My mind was racing as I anticipated the cause of the decline in culture.

Quite frankly, even though my mind was racing, I wasn't extremely concerned. I knew the culture was solid, I knew we had the right people on the team, and I knew the business was headed in the right direction. But I also knew things were really busy at the time and culture can take a hit when people feel overwhelmed. So I already knew before the words came out of her mouth that we would have things back on track in no time. I leaned back and waited for the culprit of the culture theft to be revealed.

Kristy stammered, "Well, the issue is . . . Well . . . ummm . . . It's *you*."

I wish I had the words to explain my experience in that situation. It felt like I just got hit by a truck. Kristy's uneasiness walking into my office; her shaky voice when it is normally full of confidence; the preset appointment to talk about this instead of just popping into my office—it all made sense now. She had to courageously step into her boss's office as a representative of multiple people on her team to basically say, "Hey boss... you're kinda sucking it up here." That is not what she said, nor what she meant, but that's exactly how it felt.

For the next several minutes my mind didn't race; it didn't try to solve the problem; it didn't try to anticipate how this came about. I simply sat quietly and listened.

Without question, this was the worst moment in my professional career. On the other hand, it is quite possibly the moment I am most thankful for in my professional career. As I listened to Kristy, I took in all of her and her team's feedback. While I felt like I was under siege to a degree, I was so proud of Kristy. She was articulate, organized, and gave reasons for her assertions followed by great examples. She handled the conversation like a true professional. It was an awesome moment for me to see her growth and development taking place right before my eyes. I just wish the topic would have been something different!

Taking It Like a Leader

If you're like me at all, you have a lot of questions at this point. You picked this book up off the shelf to read about how to transform your business, your team, or even just yourself into a servant leader creating a culture that thrives. Now you just read that the author of the book got called out by a team member for hurting the culture. Before you demand a refund or burn the book, let me break down some of the findings that I learned that day and how we approached these issues as a team. Then if you still want to burn the book or demand a refund, go for it.

When we opened the business back in 2005 we had three owners: my mom, my dad, and myself. We had one hired team member in addition to the original three. From the early planning stages, to the site selection, construction decisions, grand opening date, training plan—you name it, right from the beginning the three of us acted as a unified group of owners. We all had different responsibilities within the business, but we were in sync when it came to how we were going to run it, what big decisions to make, and most importantly the culture we wanted to set, grow and maintain within the team.

Fast forward twelve years and all of this was still very true. The roles had shifted multiple times over the years, but with fourteen team members on board, the three of us were a unified front when it came to the ownership and conduct of the business. In addition, my parents were very active in the business for all of those twelve years. They were personally inside the business 50+ hours per week, and very hands-on. My dad was still involved in some sales; he had a keen eye for making sure the facility stayed spotless; he would make deliveries to our customers daily; and most importantly he was always there to encourage and listen to our team members. Dad was truly one of the best on the planet in caring about people, making them feel important and encouraged, but still holding them to a high standard.

My mom, well she did it all. 50 feet up in the air in a boom lift applying over 1,000 square feet of vinyl graphics on the front of the local arena? No problem. If you needed a car wrapped, she was your go-to. If production was backed up, someone would call out, "Judy!!!!" "I'm coming!," she would quickly respond. Meanwhile she was paying the bills, managing QuickBooks and handling payroll as well.

In addition to all the amazing things I didn't know my mom could do, there was one thing more I learned about her: once we opened our doors and started this journey, I had to share my mom. My mom quickly became the shop mom. We had team members with family on the other side of the state, and when things were tough for that team member, guess who they went to for "mom questions?" Who do you think went to Costco to get all the snacks and drinks? Yep, my mom. But more important than all the "mom" tasks she did so well was the intangible mom support that was so critical to our business.

I'm still convinced I have the greatest mom in the world, so sharing her with our other team members was less of a burden than a delight. I was and am so proud of her. For others to be able to have her in their court, lending a listening ear or dispensing sound advice, that was the best thing for our team.

Originally my parents had planned to be part of the business for five years. But we were having so much fun together and growing so fast that somehow five years turned into twelve years. However, the day did finally come for them to hang up the cleats. This was well communicated and well planned out between the three of us, but also with our entire team. My wife, Erin, entered the business three months prior to their retirement to take over accounts payable, QuickBooks and payroll. However the three of us committed that she would not have to be involved in any aspect of the sales or operations of the business. We did not want to have her get sucked in the areas of the business that became all-consuming. We wanted to make sure that the lines of our home life and our business life didn't get blurred. (Quite honestly, they were blurred enough as it was, so we set those boundaries in place.) We also contracted another individual to take care of deliveries three days per week. I took over some of the larger accounts my dad was working on and continued the relationship he had started.

When it came to making sure we had all of the boxes checked, we were covered. Mission accomplished.

At the time they retired, I was very active as a salesperson on our team. Most of the sales I did were at the clients' locations. My calendar was full, so there was no doubt that the transition to more administration would put more on my plate, but I felt it was nothing I couldn't handle. In our franchise business model, it is not uncommon for the owner of the business to also be an active outside salesperson; that's par for the course and nothing to raise concern.

So when my parents transitioned out of the business, I was out of the office even more than when my parents were in the business. However, I knew we had a great team with lots of veteran team members, a strong culture, and a great work ethic that didn't need to be micromanaged. So there shouldn't have been any issue. Right?

When my parents were active in the business, it was a rare day when all three of us were out of the building at the same time. In fact, I would dare say that there was a Gilpin in the building 95 percent of the time we were open for business. There were a couple of family vacations we took over the years where all of us were gone at the same time, but outside of those instances, one of us at a minimum was present and accounted for inside the building when our doors were open.

When we made the transition, mom and dad were retired and living in Florida. Erin, while she is a Gilpin, managed to accomplish the tasks assigned to her in a couple half-days during the week. As mentioned previously, we put boundaries around her responsibilities, and while she loves the people on our team, she was focused just on those few things. Get in, get it done, get out. So we went from three owners inside the building 95 percent of the time to one owner spending 20 percent of his time inside the building based on my schedule. Yikes!

Back to Kristy's feedback. In summary, it boiled down to these three things:

1. You are never around.
2. You are focused more on the numbers than the people.
3. You are unapproachable when you are around because you're so busy.

All of the specific issues she raised that were not related to these three things could be directly tied back to my lack of presence and availability with the team.

This feedback made me sick to my stomach. Me??? More focused on the numbers than the people?!? That is exactly who I try NOT to be. Not approachable? Approachability is part of my DNA. It is part of who I want to be, and I value these people. As for my never being around, well that one felt about right. I was exhausted, burning the candle at both ends and just trying to keep this growing business on the right track.

When Kristy finished her list of things to talk about, I thanked her. We shed a couple tears as it was hard for me to hear and hard for her to say, but we both knew at that moment that it was needed.

I ended up grabbing my keys and going for a drive, one that involved a lot more than just a couple of tears. I was devastated. I wasn't being criticized for not being good at any specific task; I was being criticized for not showing that I care. Those who know me well might think that this criticism was misguided or came from a disgruntled individual rather than the team; it was anything but factual. However, as I continued on that drive, with tears streaming down my checks, I knew she was right. I wasn't around. I was outwardly showing my stress in a way that would keep someone from feeling like they could come to me with a question, and with the approach of becoming a top 5 center out of the 700+ centers in the country, we were after the numbers.

I couldn't believe that I had let things get so out of hand. And the worst part was that I didn't even realize it. The people that helped build this business and that I cared so deeply about were not getting the best version of myself.

Formulating a Plan for Change

I didn't even have to get all the way back from my drive to know that change was going to happen. It was going to be good, and we were not just going to get the culture back to where it had been. No, it was going to be even better. So I took a hard hit on the chin; it was an unexpected hit, but feedback creates growth, and an effective leader learns to listen and adapt. I was bound and determined to show to my team that I had heard their feedback and that I was ready to make positive changes. I owed as much to all of them.

When I pulled into the parking lot, I made my way into my office and I started writing down notes from my conversation with Kristy. I sent her a note and laid out my next steps. First, I wanted to take time to digest everything she said, put it down on paper and recap it to her to make sure I didn't miss anything she or the team were trying to say. It was an emotional conversation, and I didn't want to take a chance of missing a key component of this feedback.

Since the majority of the feedback to Kristy came from the sales team, the next order of business was to recap with that group to make sure they knew that their voices were being heard, and to clarify with them that I understood what they were trying to say.

With those initial steps complete, the next was a full company meeting highlighting my shortcomings, but more importantly putting forth an action plan to ensure that my availability and presence with the team was going to change for the better. I ended up scheduling one-on-one meetings with every team member, every week. While I knew it was not sustainable to keep up sixteen weekly meetings, I had to start there. I had to connect with each team member for a minimum of fifteen minutes a week to understand their highs and lows of the week as well as listening to anything they wanted to share.

I learned a lot, but most importantly they learned that I was there for them. These brief meetings also reconnected me with each person so they didn't need to make a scheduled meeting with me to know I was available to them.

The best part of all this was that within six months the team let me know that our company culture was better than it had ever been before. There were many factors that went into this change, but none of it would have happened had Kristy not come to me and given me the worst—and the best— day in my professional career.

Key Takeaways

There are plenty of takeaways from this entire experience, but here are a few of the key ones:

1. *Your team needs to know they can come to you with feedback about you!* While it was not easy for Kristy to call that

meeting, she knew that she could have this conversation with me. Why? Because one of our core values is being humble enough to learn. While I know it may sound hypocritical to pat myself on the back for being humble, I do believe that leading with a humble approach is critical. I make mistakes. I own up to them. I am not better than anyone else. It is not my way or the highway. Our team knows that about me, because this is one of the values my parents and I established at the beginning. If I'm more of a dictator and never let my mistakes be known, this conversation probably never happens.

2. *Listen to major feedback; recap it to make sure you get it, and then put a plan into place.* The best way to get feedback in the future is to do something with the feedback you receive. Without follow-up action, there isn't much point in going through the process of sharing the feedback.

3. *Pick yourself up!* I don't mean to sound harsh, but if you are a leader in your business, you don't get to have pity parties. Those are reserved for others who want to partake if they choose, but not you. You may likely have to listen to pity parties over the years, but you don't get to have one. Pick yourself up, make a plan, communicate it well, and get after it.

Finally, remember that what may seem to be your worst day could actually turn into your best day as a leader, as a professional, as a small business owner, and as a person.

CHAPTER 10
YOU CAN'T FIND GOOD PEOPLE

I'M NOT EXACTLY SURE WHEN the phrase "you can't find good people" started becoming so prevalent, but by 2020, prior to the COVID-19 pandemic, it was a common phrase.

And it seemed to come up in all kinds of different situations. At any social gathering, it seemed like this topic would arise quickly. Instead of "How about this weather we're having?", I heard "Isn't this world filled with worthless people that don't want to work?"

Not only would I hear this in social settings, but also in business networking groups, and even quite frequently at our annual conference. In those situations, this topic tended to dominate conversation: it was all about the lazy millennials, people with a sense of entitlement, lack of drive, nonexistent work ethic, people's demands for time off... "My goodness, it's like having a job is an inconvenience to their busy lives!" I've heard it all.

And while I would observe and listen in on these conversations, I would always dread that one moment when someone would say, "Hey Mike, you're a business owner, you know what it's like, right?" Ugh. I was called out. I was asked to join the commiserating. But of course, I couldn't.

In these situations, I try to take one of two approaches. If the people I'm talking to just want to complain and really don't care what anyone else has to say as long as they got to say their peace, I typically respond with "We must have gotten lucky; our entire team is pretty strong." I usually feel bad leaving those conversations knowing I just told a white lie, but there are times I just don't feel like ruffling the feathers of people who want to have a good, senseless pity party.

However, sometimes when I'm in these conversations I see a glimmer of hope that the people talking are looking at themselves in the mirror. That's when I'm "all in" on having a different conversation.

No Good People?

In order to set the table for this conversation, I need to address the rumor floating out there. Let's take a look at that statement: "There are no good people out there who want to work." Ok, stop it. For real. Now, if you are an extremely large business that is opening a plant in a new area and you need to make 2500 hires to get the plant going, you have some different challenges. But, if you are a small to midsize business owner, my guess is that at any given time you are likely looking to hire one, two or no more than ten people.

Take a look at the population of your town or city, and also look at the population of your county and neighboring counties. Are you telling me that there are actually less than ten people out there who are "good people who want to work?" We can get into all kinds of discussion regarding the changes in the labor force over the years and generations, but the fact is, there *are* good people all over the place who want to work hard and work well. So, if you are one who finds yourself saying something contrary, stop. You're feeding your mind (and likely your entire team's mind) with rhetoric that is not healthy if you truly want to build a strong team. Negativity breeds more negativity, so do yourself a favor and turn that kind of thinking around.

You may argue that back in the day you could throw a job opening out there and your inbox would be flooded with resumes. Now you throw one up on Indeed and they only trickle in. It used to be so much easier to find people: To this point I will concede. If you want to say it is harder now than it was before, that's fine, I'll give you that. You know what else is harder than it used to be? Keeping up with technology, meeting the response-time expectations of customers, managing supply chains, and competing with online retailers. Just because something is harder doesn't mean that it can't be done. There is a difference between knowing that finding the next best hire for your organization is going to be a challenge and believing that it's impossible.

Hiring Good People

Let me first address why changing this negative mentality is so critical. First of all, it forces you to lower the bar. If you say you find it impossible to find good people, then you happen to interview someone who has some good experience but seems arrogant and probably not a culture fit for your organization, you may well think, "Well shoot, since good people are hard to find, I'd better hire this person before they find another job."

This mentality creates desperation. Desperation leads to hires that are not the right fit for your organization. Once this hire, who wasn't a good fit to start with, integrates into your organization, guess how long he's there? My guess is he's there as long as he wants to be. Why? Because you can't get rid of him! Why not? If you do, you won't be able to replace him because "there are no good people who are willing to work" out there! You see how this kind of thinking can create a negative spiral?

If you settle on a hire, you'll likely settle on keeping that hire on your team even if he or she isn't a fit. Repeat that a few times and you don't exactly have the work environment you were hoping to build. And when the work environment goes downhill, productivity, quality and creativity are sure to follow.

So, please, don't believe the myth. There absolutely *are* good people out there.

Now that we have established that there are good people who want to work, here is the question to ask: Instead of focusing on why you would want them to join your team, ask yourself, why would this person want to join my team? Flip the script, take a look in the mirror, and humble yourself enough to be open to learning more about you and your organization. This process takes quite a bit of reflection.

Quite often I hear from others that their pay structures are competitive—that's why someone would want to join their team. Don't get me wrong, I'm all in favor of paying people well, but if this is the leading reason why a candidate should join your team, and it matches their top reason for joining your team, you can guess what comes next. If joining a team is all about the pay, then that person will likely always be for sale.

Too often the pay package is the driving factor in trying to win over a candidate. But let's just take the pay package out of the equation for a moment. What will make this person look forward to pulling into the parking lot every Monday morning? Why will they want to go the extra mile when they join your team? What is it about their job or the company they work for that is going to make them want to tell their friends and family about where they spend the majority of their waking hours?

It's critical to create a work environment that sets and builds vision, direction, purpose, teamwork, community giving, social rewards, financial rewards, acknowledgment, accolades, accountability, growth potential, and a feeling among team members that their voice matters. When you as a leader bundle this kind of culture with a good pay package, that's when you have something that will have your team members looking forward to pulling into that parking lot on a Monday morning.

Seeking individuals to join your team who will work *with* you and not *for* you can make all the difference in the world. If you have a team that has built momentum by authentically caring for one another, pushing each other toward being better today than they were yesterday, and showing a level of commitment to each other and the company, it will draw other talent in.

One of the positive characteristics of the younger generations coming up is their desire to be a part of something special. They want to spend their time being a part of something with purpose. Interpersonal connections are very important to them. Belonging to a tribe is something that matters to them, and you have the opportunity in your business to create such a tribe.

Culture Motivates: Be Honest

Now you may be reading this thinking that you don't have the culture that you want, so you can't sell that to an interview candidate. If that's true of you, the big question you have to face is, do you know what culture shift you want to see happen? And a related question is, have you shared your vision with your existing team?

If you have, then that same vision can be shared with a potential candidate. The fear of scaring them away because things are a little rough at the moment needs to go away. Too often when potential employers sugarcoat a company's issues, the new team member will learn within days (if not hours) what the corporate culture is really like. So in the interview process, don't sugarcoat anything; lay your cards on the table and be honest. If you don't you'll likely see candidates find the exit door just as quickly as they found the entry door.

No potential hire is expecting to walk into a perfect company without any issues, so don't pretend that's what you're offering. It isn't. There are inefficiencies, ongoing challenges, and improvements to be made in your business. Just be real about it.

If you have a culture that is tracking, or one that you are really proud of, be sure to include your great people not only in the interview process, but also in the recruiting process. Use your team's network of connections to try and find the next great teammate you can bring on board.

At FASTSIGNS 467 We are in a fortunate position: we have built a team where people from the outside have heard about our culture, they have seen what we do as a team, and they want in!

It is humbling to know that we have people leaving our competitors to come to our team and join the growth we are experiencing.

Two recent applicants came to us because they were looking for things that we offer in our shop: better communication, a clear vision of the path forward, acknowledgment of the good work they do, a listening ear for their ideas, and simply to be valued as a human being. Both were hired and have been with us for a year now. And I still wonder why their previous employer couldn't show up for them. What they were looking for was not unreasonable: All they were asking for was some basic respect, appreciation and communication. Yet many small business owners who expect their employees to show up every day for them don't reciprocate by showing up for their employees.

Employment, when done well, is all about partnership. Every single hire, regardless of the level of qualification required or where the position sits on an organizational chart, should be viewed as a partner in your business. Regardless of the number of "good people who want to work" are out there, I can guarantee there are more than enough looking to join a team where they feel like a partner and valued for who they are and what they can bring to the table.

CHAPTER 11
POP QUIZ? NOPE . . . POP EXAM!

IN MARCH OF 2020 our world was crippled with the COVID-19 virus. In many aspects, the world shut down in a monumental effort to keep the deadly virus from spreading.

While it was a heated topic then, now, and likely will be for years and years to come, I am not here to discuss the way the pandemic was handled. Regardless of your personal views, I think there is a genuine consensus that it was one of the most difficult times in our country's history. Nearly everyone I know was connected to someone who nearly lost their life or did lose their life from the virus. I would be remiss to not acknowledge the tragedy this brought to so many. My focus in this chapter will be from the small business perspective and is not intended to come across as callous or unaware of the personal difficulty so many families went through because of the global pandemic.

The Pandemic and 467

When this pandemic hit, things happened that I never would have dreamed would come about: government mandates shutting schools and businesses down; restricted hours for grocery shopping; medical procedures canceled indefinitely; country borders closing. It was intense, it was surreal, and we were in a full-on war with an invisible virus. Again, one can debate the relative effectiveness of these policies, but those were the cards we were dealt—right, wrong or indifferent.

Many times as a small business owner you can feel like the deck is stacked against you, but under these conditions that's probably the biggest understatement I can think of. At 467, we were in an all-out fight for our survival. While we pride ourselves in planning ahead, casting a vision, working toward a goal, all of those good intentions and effective planning changed in an instant. We went from focusing on our 12-week goals to figuring out how to attack the next twelve hours.

As of March 13, 2020, I was operating as the CEO of our business and spending more and more time *on* the business and less and less time *in* the business. As of March 16, 2020, I was 100 percent focused on nothing but things in the business. Everything was focused on TODAY, and if we were in a really good spot today, we might even consider what tomorrow may bring.

I spent endless hours reading through executive orders from our state. Can we stay open? Are we essential services? And as for the PPP Loan, do we qualify? Who is the best to use for the application process? Should we use the recommended national lender or trust our local bank? Will the money run out before everyone gets what they need for this shutdown period?

And what about health and safety protocols? They changed every day. Are masks required, and if so, what type? How many people can be in the building at one time? What is required for a health check for those coming to work each day? More than just a temperature check? What method is needed for documenting this? And what about the process if someone contracts COVID-19?

Oh, and even more confusing, what if your mom was over at your sister's house and your nephew was there as well and you just found out your nephew's daycare teacher tested positive for COVID, but your mom was just at your house last night? It was like playing six degrees of Kevin Bacon every single day. Now that we connected all the dots and you might have been exposed, what is the quarantine period? Is it ten days or fourteen days? The CDC says one thing, the WHO says another thing, but our state says something else.

Who can work from home, and will that be effective? Small businesses had less than a week to figure out how to get their information technology infrastructure set up to have people work from home. Of course I could go on and on, and likely you who are reading this are remembering way too many horror stories that could only add to this list of the challenges we faced.

With that said, we were in a heated battle, and the thought of trying to figure out our third-quarter marketing plan or our next piece of equipment to add to our capabilities quickly became laughable. My focus changed to the day-to-day triage of the business which created a 796-day pause in this book writing process. While there weren't 796 actual days of triage, it did take that long to finally feel like I was back into the mindset of being able to focus on something other than our FASTSIGNS business in my working hours.

Thankfully, the vaccine emerged and since that time life has returned to a new normal. While we at 467 have not been in the triage mode for quite some time, it was still an adjustment for me to be able to get to the point where I could put pen to paper again.

However, as we've learned before, sometimes the worst experiences can turn into your best learning experiences. I couldn't be more thankful for this 796-day pause in writing.

While I would never want to go through a pandemic again, I will admit that during the process we learned a lot. The best way I can put it is that we were all given the most enormous "pop quiz" in the life of our business.

Remember the "pop quiz"? I sure do. I remember walking into class and the teacher saying she's going to give a "pop quiz" on the reading that she assigned last night. I didn't know there was going to be a quiz. If there had been a planned quiz, I could have made a conscious decision to prepare for it. We all know that a pop quiz is designed to test your level of preparedness at any point in time.

When the pandemic hit, it wasn't really a "pop quiz," it was more like a "pop thorough examination of all aspects of the health of your business: finances, personnel, communication, procedures, culture, supply chain, customer relations and the will to win/survive." This was an examination like we've never experienced before. This was the final exam of the toughest class ever, and many approached it with the pass-fail mentality.

Our team took a different approach: We didn't want to just pass the exam, we wanted to ace it. We didn't just want to survive the pandemic, we wanted to thrive. We didn't want to just make it through, we wanted to be stronger on the other side of it. While I am not sure we can say that the pandemic is over, we are far closer to back to normal than we have been in a long time at the time of this writing. And with that, we at 467 have received our grade. We aced it.

While we were far from perfect, we are stronger on this side of the pandemic. As a team we pulled together and experienced great success, and now our future is brighter than ever before. We didn't know we were going to be tested like this, but we were prepared.

The entire premise of this book, "We Before Me," is the top reason for our success. I used to think that company culture was needed because people deserve it and it gives more purpose to the work we do. What I didn't know, and what I definitely know now, is that company culture also creates one of the greatest security blankets you could ask for when "you-know-what" hits the fan.

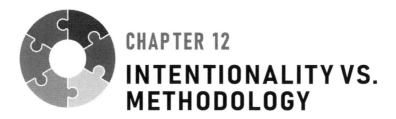

CHAPTER 12
INTENTIONALITY VS. METHODOLOGY

AS YOU HAVE MADE YOUR WAY through this book, you probably surmised it is not a step-by-step instruction manual on implementing a strong culture within your business. Quite frankly, I don't believe something like that exists. If you are looking to become more efficient with your time, get things out of your head so you can be more present in the moment, and overall make sure you are spending your time at work in the most appropriate areas, I would highly recommend David Allen's book *Getting Things Done: The Art of Stress-Free Productivity.*[4] It is a great book that includes a step-by-step methodology you can follow to implement the philosophy he promotes.

Perhaps you are looking to structure your business in a way that creates better communication, more clearly defined core values, shared one-year, three-year and 10-year goals, and are interested in putting an accountability system in

[4] Penguin Books, 2015, ISBN 9780143126560

place. If so, implementing the EOS (Entrepreneurial Operating System) outlined in the book *Traction: Get a Grip on Your Business*[5] by Gino Wickman would be a great place to start. Wickman describes proven methods toward achieving these goals using step-by-step procedures to provide a road map to follow to get you to the place you want to go. *Traction* gives readers almost a recipe to follow so that steps are implemented in a certain order. Implementing this plan within your business is easy to follow because of that recipe for success.

Unfortunately, a similar playbook does not exist for creating a "We Before Me" environment that resembles the team at 467. There's a reason why I've shared personal examples in the chapters preceding this one. It's because (yep you guessed it) culture is personal! Very personal!

Intentionality rather than methodology is what will create the culture you desire. Being intentional is by far the most effective way to build into people, to make them feel valued, and to empower them to spread their wings and fly. Can some of what we've experienced at 467 be laid out within a business plan, follow some step-by-step actions to move the culture along, and have some metrics to follow to know if you are making progress? Yes. However, I would say that all of that pales in comparison to the importance of the team's frame of mind and the intentionality behind what you're doing.

As a team, you have to know what you're doing, when you're doing it, and why you're doing it. Opportunities to improve and deepen a culture don't usually show up announced; you have to be ready. And this is about the team: it is about people, and it is about valuing them for who they are as human beings.

---

[5] BenBella Books, 2012, ISBN 9781936661831

We have twenty different human beings on our team. Just because there are two guys in production that run the same equipment, that doesn't make them the same in how they want to be treated, how they are motivated, or how they best feel part of the team. Culture incorporates the unique differences of each team member and adapts to create the best environment for the team. That involves intentionality, communication, humility, and a clear feedback loop.

467 Summary

Even though I'm not putting forth a certain methodology directed toward implementing or improving a company culture, I can still summarize what has been shared here to help refresh your frame of mind. When a leader's frame of mind is in the right place, intentionality in words and actions is at the ready. So, here is a rundown of what we covered.

Know Your Why

You have to figure this out. If you don't know why you want to be a leader or why you want to own the business, you are missing out. While running a business can be done without this kind of meta-thinking, when it is, the owner simply misses out on defining what the great purpose is behind the hours upon hours they pour into their business on a daily basis. Don't shortcut this one. Figure it out. If you know your why, write it down.

Team Members > Customers

Every one of your team members is more important than any of your customers. Maybe you've not had this thought before and it is thought provoking. Perhaps you've thought about it and agree that it is more critical to be of service to your team member than to any of your customers. Now the question is, where is your intentionality directed?

While it's great to understand this concept in theory, think about what you're doing to live this out on a daily basis. This is a great example of why there is no preset formula for success in this regard. Do you treat all of your customers the same? If not, you're not likely to treat all of your team members the same either. Former NFL coach Tony Dungy once said, "I need to treat everyone fairly, but fair doesn't always mean equal." It is very much the same with your internal customers: each one has different needs, and what you do to try and help satisfy those needs will look different in each case.

Exceed Your External Customers' Expectations

Remember, deep down your team wants to exceed their customers' expectations and perform well in their work. It is part of the human DNA, and your job is to help pull this impulse out of your team members on a daily basis. Again, what this looks like will change based on the industry and the customer, but the focus on exceeding expectations needs to be intentionally a part of your conversation. When it catches on, it becomes part of your culture.

The best testimony you will have that this is working is when you bring new people on the team and they're surprised at how you go above and beyond for a customer. What's more, they will soon realize that their fellow team members have an instant sense of pride in the company they work for and the products and services they produce. Because not many companies are being intentional about this critical aspect of their business, this creates low-hanging fruit for your company as you strive to stand out from your competitors and impress this mindset to your new team members.

Hire Smart and Hire Well

What are you really looking for in a new team member? Is it that perfect resume with all of the boxes checked? As shared previously, Tom was willing to bring a sleeping bag to work and sleep by the cutting equipment if needed. Thankfully, that still has never been needed, but that level of "above and beyond" thinking far exceeded any software experience he had under his belt or product knowledge he was bringing to the table.

I don't know what the person coming through the door to the next interview at your organization will bring, but if you are intentional in looking past the resume highlights and checked boxes, you may get to know something about that person that can give you a better indication of how they would gel with the chemistry of your team.

Skills are nice, but most can be taught. Finding the right person is more important than finding the right applicant. Yes, I shared our methodology on hiring, but it is your intentionality behind how you hire that will create your own process (or feel free to steal ours!)

Find Purpose in Your Work

Nick's story is a great one. I love what he brings to our team and I love that it is recognized. And you probably already know what I am going to say, but I have to say it anyway: Identifying the purpose in Nick's work on our team took intentionality. By recognizing that purpose, Nick had a chance to build on it and become a more effective teammate, which is wonderful. But what is even more wonderful, he truly enjoyed what he was doing even more because it was so much more than just "making signs."

If you have team members who see the great purpose in the work they're doing, support it, encourage it and try to get behind it in any way you can. If you have team members who only see their purpose as managing the task at hand, help them see their greater purpose. Again, every organization and person within the organization will be different, so there is no formula for establishing this kind of perspective. But with the right intentionality, you will find this purpose.

The Seats on the Bus

Tim was the right guy to have on the bus; he was just in the wrong seat. Fourteen months of working through his desire to transfer may still sound crazy to some people, but we did it together. There was not a set formula we were following, but we were both being intentional about seeking the next steps to get us on a path to create a happier, healthier career for Tim. In the process, we ensured that we had great talent in the right seat on the bus.

The best way to be intentional in this area is to be open. If someone is in the wrong seat, that's ok! Hopefully there is a way to fix it, or perhaps adjustments are just needed within that same seat to make the ride a little better. And while it is never easy, sometimes the next best move for a team member is to be dropped off at the bus stop so they can find a great seat on another bus. Having the right people on the bus in the right seats can be a fluid experience. Be open to it!

Don't Be Afraid to Address Tough Situations

When I delivered the team's feedback to Wesley, she was crushed. There's no other way to say it: it sucked. Having that conversation is tough, and knowing what's coming is an awful feeling.

There are those who are better than me at sharing bad news, but my encouragement to you if you're preparing to do something similar is to look past the difficult encounter. Look six months down the road. While that conversation will always be a difficult one when looking in the rearview mirror, how much better will the future of your team be if you have the conversation now?

Yes, Wesley was a special person to take on the challenge and make changes, but too often team members never get the chance to show they can take on the challenge because it is too uncomfortable to challenge them. Be prepared, be professional, but share the news. It's not mean, it's clear.

Look in the Mirror

If there is feedback coming your way that is negative, check all of your defense mechanisms at the door. Here is the frame of mind and intentionality to have in these situations: Someone on your team thinks you can be better! That's great news!

Do you honestly think you're the absolute best leader on the planet with no room for improvement? Of course not! So, why not take on feedback directed toward you with a sense of encouragement that someone believes you can be even better than you are today? Most importantly be intentional by making sure your team knows that this feedback is welcomed and allowed.

Final Summary

"We Before Me" is first and foremost a mentality. Once the mentality is in place, intentional words and actions create the special kind of environment that will give a team of people a reason to feel good when they pull into the parking lot on Monday morning.

Be humble, work smart, be vulnerable, and put others before yourself. When you do, you will have created something more special than you can imagine. After you pour yourself into the team, they'll start pouring themselves into each other, and that's when the magic happens—your business will thrive to new levels you could have never before imagined.

Not a bad byproduct of simply treating people the way they should be treated, right?

CHAPTER 13

MY SECRET WEAPON AND ULTIMATE ROLE MODEL

WHILE I TRULY BELIEVE the culture and success we have built at FASTSIGNS 467 is because of the team we have built and what they each contribute, I often still get peppered with questions about me personally. Every once in a while someone mentions that the team is great because they have a great leader, or some other kudos get directed toward me personally. I have had many team members share these sentiments with me as well.

And while I do appreciate these kinds of comments, I tend to deflect them away from me because, at the end of the day, I don't see what I'm doing in my role as a leader as being that special. It drives me crazy when I hear about organizations that have created toxic work environments where people are just a number and not valued for the human beings they are. To me, treating the people on your team well just makes good common sense.

I am rarely the smartest guy in the room; I am not the most creative; I don't have the best ideas; and when it comes to effective communication, I can somehow find a way to use ten words when three would do the job. Yes, I do believe I bring a lot of value to our team, but I also believe the credit I receive tends to far exceed what is appropriate. But I still get questions about me personally as a leader: how I manage to handle things the way I do, or how some of our team philosophies started. So, I thought I would open up a little bit and give you a look inside me: who I am as a person and how that has shaped my philosophies and leadership style.

The reason I've reserved this for the closing chapter is that this part is about me and my story. You may have a perspective and lifestyle that doesn't come close to reflecting mine, and that doesn't change the fact that the principles in this book still hold true.

So without further ado, the heart of Michael Gilpin: Jesus Christ. He is my secret weapon and ultimate role model.

I was raised by two amazing parents and have a sister who has become a great friend. While my sister and I never hated each other, we were never at the top of each other's list growing up either. Since then we have gained so much respect for each other, and she is a true blessing in my life. Growing up in a faith-based family, reverence and love for God was an integral part of my life. However, when I went away to Miami University in Oxford, Ohio, the faith I had became more personal; I realized that I wanted to pursue a deeper relationship in my Christian walk with God.

I met my wife our sophomore year at Miami, and we often attended meetings for Campus Crusade (now called Cru) together. I was able to get plugged into some men's Bible studies, and had a small group of guys to lean on. All along I knew that this was part of my DNA: the essence of who I was. Jesus Christ died on the cross for me, forgave me of my sins and I was "all in" to find out what my life with Him could be. When Erin and I were married and moved to Allentown, Pennsylvania, we were fortunate to find a great church to join. We made some incredible friends and had some great teaching from the senior pastor at our church.

Now, with all that said, let me make one thing very clear: My life hasn't been a perfect storybook. I had anger issues to work on, struggled with lack of follow through on my commitments to Erin, and I wasn't always the best dad I could possibly be.

Often those that don't share this faith take a look from the outside in and assume Christians and Christianity are the same thing, but they're not. Christianity is the belief that Jesus Christ is the Son of God who came to earth to die for the sins of those who are willing to trust him for salvation. Christians seek to be in a relationship with Jesus and follow what he says, but Christians totally screw up on a regular basis and then have to ask for forgiveness.

I often hear that Christians are hypocrites: they believe you should behave one way and then they do the opposite. Yep. Some much more than others, but Jesus Christ is the only perfect person who ever walked the earth, so anyone else will fall far short of perfection, even if they choose to follow Him.

Grace

One of the biggest realities that I have learned about from my faith is the amazing word, action and gift called "grace." I am saved by grace. God didn't have to save "a wretch like me," but He did. Because of the death and resurrection of His Son Jesus, I am saved not by my own works, but by His. Grace is something that I have experienced in my faith, but I've also experienced it from my wife and kids and several of my friends.

I truly believe that one of the greatest ways to show God's love to others is by showing them grace. No matter who we are, we're going to screw up. Mistakes happen. Sometimes they're not careless mistakes; rather, they are premeditated, thought-out, bad decisions that are hurtful and harmful. Many mistakes are purely innocent, but there are also plenty of times when that isn't the case.

If you were to study the time that Jesus walked the earth you would find that when He encountered the sinners of the world, He did not come at them with an iron fist; rather, He approached them with grace and love. I would like to think that if you polled our team today and asked if grace was part of my leadership style, you would get a resounding "Yes!" Many of my team members may not know where that grace stems from, but the truth is that it is truly inspired by my relationship with Jesus Christ.

You may want to quickly interject here and say that you don't have to be a Christian in order to show others grace. I agree! That is 100 percent accurate.! But, in order to share with you some of the key characteristics of why I lead the way I do, it's important that you know the source of where it comes from for me.

Servant Leadership

My team members may see me as a person who gives and receives grace. And if that's true, I would hope that they would also agree that I'm a servant leader. I love the visual of taking the organizational chart and flipping it upside down to show the order of service. I firmly believe that if you're at the top of the organizational chart, you are the one who should be serving everyone!

What is servant leadership? There are many definitions out there, but my definition is rather simple: Put the needs of others before your own needs. Simple. Effective. And... the best example of this? You guessed it, my buddy JC once again. Jesus Christ walked the earth for only a short amount of time, but his servant leadership was evident on so many levels. There are so many examples in the Bible, but I will refer to just one to help illustrate my point.

In the thirteenth chapter of the Gospel of John, Jesus entered a home for what would be his last meal before being crucified. All of his closest companions were there. So, picture this... the man, the top dog, the CEO, is strolling into the room for a dinner that is really for him.

In those days, it was customary for the servants to wash the guests' feet as they entered the home before eating a meal. The lowliest of all the servants would get this job because it was dirty and thankless. Keep in mind, these people weren't running around down in their Nike or New Balance shoes, and there wasn't a paved road around. They wore sandals and their feet got filthy, and there was quite possibly an extended time between washings. So of course, the lowliest of servants would have this job. But when Jesus arrived on this critical day and his disciples were there, he began to wash their feet!

You may have heard this story or passed over it before, but if you really stop to reflect on what is taking place here it is quite remarkable. The disciples were uncomfortable with this and asked Jesus not to do that for them because they were not worthy. They did not feel important enough to have Him washing their feet. His response was, "If I then, your Lord and Teacher, have washed your feet, you also ought to wash one another's feet. For I have given you an example, that you should do as I have done to you" (John 13:14-15). Combine this story with the statement from Matthew 20:28: "For even the Son of Man did not come to be served, but to serve . . ."

If this all-powerful Son of God, one who could have just demanded to be served and have anyone and everyone wash His feet, said, "Nope... I am going to serve you," then I have to ask myself, "Why not me?" His is an incredible example and one that inspires me to find new ways to be a servant leader. I have avoided actually washing my team members' feet, but I think you get the point.

What does being a servant leader look like? It could mean stepping in to take something off a team member's plate because they are overloaded. It could be rearranging my schedule to cover for them because their kid is sick or they have an appointment they need to go to. It could be as simple as giving a team member a listening ear and my undivided attention even though my to-do list is a little longer than I would like. It could mean simply figuring out what tools and resources my people need to do their job more effectively. How can I be there for them and service them better? That is my goal.

Humility

The third area that is a great influence comes from Philippians 2:3-4: "Do nothing out of selfish ambition or vain conceit. Rather, in humility value others above yourselves, not looking to your own interests, but each of you to the interests of others." A simple way to put this is that it is not about me.

Our pastor in Pennsylvania had a great sermon on this topic that resonated with me then and still does today. I think we have all encountered people who, no matter the situation, make everything ALL about them. That kind of person will make decisions solely based on how they will affect him or her. Yes, you do need to take yourself into consideration, but focusing only on how a decision will impact you creates blind spots for how they will impact others. I don't write this to try to anoint myself as some kind of selfless martyr, but hopefully I've made the point so you can better understand the inspiration for the "We Before Me" mantra.

Final Thoughts

Finally, the rollercoaster of being a small business owner or business leader can be intense. If you are on that roller coaster now, you know what I mean. There are highs and lows, decisions that need to be made that will keep you up all night, conflict on the team that needs to be resolved, cash flow concerns, and the list goes on and on. But that's where my faith comes in.

Part of my Christian walk is having a faith centered outside of myself that is filled with comfort, wisdom, encouragement, and peace. I may try to do it all on my own too often, but my faith has guided me through many difficult situations, and I am forever thankful for it.

Wherever you might be in your perspective on faith, if you are not familiar with the life and teachings of Jesus Christ, I would recommend taking a look. I am not here on a pulpit trying to preach, but learning about Jesus and how he handled his business here on earth, if nothing else, can lead to some great examples of leadership that will be instructive for your situation. I would encourage you to at least give it a look.

My hope at this point is that you have gained something from the pages you have read. My bigger hope is that, because you've spent some time in this book, somewhere out there is a person who is going to pull into the parking lot on Monday morning and start to have a different experience. Maybe they're dreading the work they have to do and are drained and worn out by the time they pull back out at the end of the day, but my hope is that in the weeks and months to come that drive in on Monday morning will become something to look forward to.

Remember, it is not our responsibility as leaders to pour into the lives of those we work with, it is our opportunity. It's not something we *have* to do; it's something we *get* to do.

Make the best of it and be well.